M000098962

Sink or Swim:
A Survival Story

Tammy Levent

Published by Richter Publishing LLC www.richterpublishing.com

Editors: Mandi Weems & Jenna Rimensnyder

Formatted by: Diana Fisler

Copyright © 2015 Tammy Levent

All rights reserved. In accordance with U.S. Copyright Act of 1976, the scanning, uploading, and electronic sharing of any part of this book without permission of the publisher constitute unlawful piracy and theft of the author's intellectual property. No part of this book may be reproduced in any form by any electronic or mechanical means (including photocopying, recording or information storage and retrieval) without permission in writing from the author or publisher. Thank you for your support of the author's rights.

ISBN:0692588299
ISBN-13:9780692588291

DISCLAIMER

This book is written about the author's life for entrainment only. This information is provided and sold with the knowledge that the publisher and author do not offer any legal or medical advice. In the case of a need for any such expertise, consult with the appropriate professional. This book does not contain all information available on a certain subject. This book has not been created to be specific to any individual's or organization's situation or needs. Every effort has been made to make this book as accurate as possible. However, there may be typographical and/ or content errors. Therefore, this book should serve only as a general guide and not as the ultimate source of subject information. This book contains information that might be dated and is intended only to educate and entertain. The author and publisher shall have no liability or responsibility to any person or entity regarding any loss or damage incurred, or alleged to have incurred, directly or indirectly, by the information contained in this book. You hereby agree to be bound by this disclaimer or you may return this book within the guarantee time period for a full refund. In the interest of full disclosure, this book contains affiliate links that might pay the author or publisher a commission upon any purchase from the company. While the author and publisher take no responsibility for the business practices of these companies and or the performance of any product or service, the author or publisher has used the product or service and makes a recommendation in good faith based on that experience. All characters appearing in this work have been represented as accurately as possible. Any resemblance to any other real persons, living or dead, that was not identified in this book directly, is purely coincidental.

DEDICATION

To my husband, Rob, who supports me in all that I do, and to my children Katie and Jordan, who've learned strength and resilience already. Mom, I also want to dedicate this to you too because thanks to you I have so much courage. You taught me to accept and embrace challenges both good and bad with mostly no fear.

FOREWORD

Dear Readers,

I want you to know something about someone near and dear to me: Tammy Levent. From the time we were infants, Tammy and I have been together, thanks to our parents, and have developed to be the dearest of friends. We are like brother and sister. Throughout the various stages of our lives, I have seen her grow and develop to be one of the strongest people I know. Tammy's depth as a person encompasses the full spectrum of a dynamic and loving human being and has within her the innate ability to make a positive difference in the lives of individuals, as well as enhancing organized groups. She does this with the ability to bring smiles and a joyful laughter to those who are privileged to be in her company.

Tammy has taken the talents that God has given us and multiplied them. She didn't bury them out of fear, or for the sake of convenience, or so as to not offend others by her confidence. She didn't allow the misunderstood notion of humility to mean that she should remain silent and non-threatening. Indeed the true meaning of the word humility is better understood from its root word "humus" which means "fertility". Tammy has the fertile mind and character where the seeds of knowledge, experience, and wisdom have grown and have yielded an abundant harvest that she happily shares with those who would like to hear. Another way to put it is that humility is "truth", and pride is "falsehood". Tammy is as true as can be. She is an agent of truth. The nature of truth is threatening to some. It exposes pretention and delusion with the refreshing light of candor, forthrightness, and genuine concern.

You might think I am biased in sharing these thoughts with you. Well, I am biased. I love her. But the reason I love her is the same reason you will love her: she has genuine character. There is nothing artificial about her. What means a lot to me is the smile of someone that has been banged-up by life. What means a lot to me is the smile of someone that has suffered the brunt of the storms of life, and still has the capacity to smile, laugh, live, and love. Tammy is this person. Gold is tempered by going through the blast-furnace of fire. It is only then that it can shine. Tammy has gone through the blast furnace of life and is able to effortlessly shine a resilient and bright smile that is contagious. That is the kind of person I want to be around.

- **George N. Patides**

Mother Teresa wrote once that we are all God's pencils that He uses to write His love letter to us. Tammy is an indelible magic marker whose message will resonate with you for years to come.

- **George N. Patides**

My mom taught me one of the most important things needed for success in life, to believe that I could do anything if I tried. If you don't try you'll fail, if you don't believe in yourself, no one else will, and believing in yourself also means believing you can help others achieve success. Nothing gets in her way, she overcomes the odds and continues to be a respected role model. She also taught me how to be a strong independent woman and of course a great cook! Love you, Mommy!

- Katie Levent

Thank you for being such an amazing mentor, friend, and most importantly mother. I hope one day my kids look up to me like I've looked up to you my whole life. I owe who I am today to you. When I think of strength and courage I think of you, mom. Thank you for always being a rock in my life where I can turn for support. Love you!

- Jordan Levent

PROLOGUE

I have always felt like I have a purpose in life. I want to leave a legacy of the importance of teaching others. My hope is that others will learn from experiences in life to help guide others to carry on.

Ever since I was a little girl, I was like a sponge gathering things I would need in life along my way. You soak everything up, but to soak up more eventually you have to let go of some shit. The things I have no use for, I let go. But my past has a lot to do with where I'm going and where I am today.

The things that have happened to me in my lifetime have molded me into a survivor. My grandmother's guidance, the things my mother taught me, what I saw in my grandparents, my experiences raising my children, even the things I saw in my biological father, and and the man that raised me that I call my father—all of these people added pieces to who I am.

My mom and my real dad – they started with nothing and became millionaires. Then, just as fast as those riches came, my dad up and left taking everything from us when I was just 14. Barely in my teens and my mom and I were left with nothing and no place to live.

No matter what happened in our lives, we were survivors, and that's the main thing I learned from my immigrant parents and grandparents, from my entrepreneurial parents, the mistakes they made – and everything I've been through (which has been a lot)—is how to survive. I always say there is no such thing as failure, it is all a learning experience and a passage called life and this is my story of surviving everything life has thrown at me.

Tammy Levent

Table of Contents

PART 1: ROLE MODELS

When I was just a toddler, maybe two or three years old, my parents would host weekly parties on their yacht, aptly named the Sea Orgy, in New York. While other parents might have hired a babysitter, mine would tie me on the end of a rope and throw me into the water. My choices were sink or swim, and somehow I always bobbed to the surface, smiling.

I was born in 1962. My birth name is Stamatia Kavourakis of the Greek side of Jamaica, Queens in New York. Stamatia was my paternal grandmother's name —which was the name everyone knew me by as I was growing up until I changed my name to the name I have today-Tammy Levent. More on that later in this story. The people who lived in our neighborhood were all Greek and Italian immigrants.

Adults: My grandfather, mother & on the bottom kneeling my grandmother

My grandparents, for the most part, raised me, partly because my parents left the house at four o'clock in the morning every day to work in our family restaurant located in the heart of Manhattan. Much of who I am today comes directly from my Yiayia's strength and kindness, characteristics she honed through war and deprivation. (For those of you who don't know, Yiayia means grandmother in Greek.)

My mother, Kay, was born in Thesaloniki, Greece in 1936. Her father, Panagiotis Gavokostas was drafted in the army in 1938 when she was just 2 years old. My YiaYia Evlambia was pregnant at the time. Sadly, my grandfather was killed in action in the Albanian war in 1939. My YiaYia gave birth to a baby boy she named Kosta that same year. World War II started in Greece the following year and the lack of food took Kosta from her at the age of two. By the ripe age of 22, my YiaYia had lost both her husband and son, and felt her dreams and future were destroyed by war.

YiaYia Evlambia was a Red Cross nurse and after the loss of her husband many people encouraged her to get married again. Her nephew introduced her to, and ultimately married a man named Vagelis. Vagelis also fought in the war and suffered from ongoing complications from a leg wound. Doctors amputated the leg, but the remaining tissue kept getting gangrene, so they continued cutting more and more. By the end of those two years, my grandparents had come to depend on each other, bonded by loss.

My grandfather was an andartes (a guerrilla fighter). He and my YiaYia married in March of 1946, but just days after the wedding he was thrown in jail for being an andartes and was accused of being a communist. After his release, he told YiaYia that he was actually born in the United States and that he was a Greek-American. So, the American Embassy helped my grandparents and mom come to America. When they arrived at Ellis Island, they moved to Harlem. I grew up with my grandmother telling me stories of how she'd save her nickel for the bus every day by walking miles to and from work in order to buy her small family food.

My YiaYia was a lady with priorities. Years later, she would buy her first house in Queens, and then her second home in Florida, with cash. From her, I learned to be frugal and wise with money, but generous to those who had less. From my grandfather, I learned kindness and how to let things go.

My grandfather owned a hotdog truck which he'd take into the ghetto of New York every day of the week. I was allowed to go with him on the weekends and after school, which was always a special treat because my grandfather seemed to know everybody. In one of these neighborhoods, his "regular customer" was a little girl just a little older than I was, maybe seven or eight years old, who was black and blind. He would always give her free hot dogs. One weekend, I asked if I could go play with her, and my grandfather said "Of course!" I walked with her back to her apartment; with her confidently tapping her stick from side to side on the pavement, knowing the way by heart. But when we walked through her front door and she introduced me, her mother started screaming at her that she couldn't keep getting free hotdogs because she was blind. To this day, I remember every word that mother screamed at her daughter: "You have to work for everything you have. No handouts just because you're blind!". I believe my grandfather gave her those hotdogs because he was handicapped himself.

My grandparents' home was a refuge, not just for me and my grandfather, but for homeless people my YiaYia would find on the street or from church. She had a huge heart, taking in strangers, feeding them, and letting them live in the attic or the basement. YiaYia had done the same in the war and saw no reason to stop in New York. I remember one man, Alex, a schizophrenic who lived in the basement, collected screws. I remember sitting there and sorting screws with him for hours. Another man she brought into the house was a quadriplegic who had lost both arms and both legs, and she worked extra shifts to buy him prosthetics while he lived in a large closet off the dining room. Years later, when I traveled to Greece as an adult in 1998, I went to his village to find out what happened to him. I met him at his tiny newsstand, and when he recognized me, he told me that if it hadn't been for my grandmother, he wouldn't have a life, much less his own small business.

As I helped my YiaYia prepare traditional Greek meals for the house, pungent with garlic and oregano, she told me I could do anything, be anything – all in Greek because she didn't speak a word of English. She was strict and rigid, always to the point and brutally honest, but true to heart—all of the characteristics she had I find in myself.

During most of the summers of my childhood, when my parents weren't working at the restaurant, they would travel to Greece, leaving me with my grandparents. One summer, my mother was looking for a summer camp to send me to and saw Forrest Hills Orthodox Day Camp. Believing Forrest Hill Day Camp was Greek Orthodox, she insisted I go. When I came home the first day and told her it was *Jewish* Orthodox, her reply was "Same thing!" and back I went.

My biological father was like the Elvis of Greece, a famous recording artist and actor with gold records and screaming fans. When my parents met, he was married with three children (who he left back in Greece). Nonetheless, my mom was star-struck and infatuated with him.

My mother was a junior in high school and my biological father was 29. She started secretly seeing him without anyone knowing for a while. Then, she went to a family function and everyone recognized my mother from seeing her in the club where my dad was performing. She knew he was already married with kids, but I think she was desiring the freedom to go out with him because of her strict upbringing. She threw caution to the wind and fell hard for him not realizing that she was actually trading in a strict upbringing for a man who would begin completely controlling her life from that day on. My mom and dad

Me and my brother Tony

quickly married without the approval of my grandparents, and without my dad divorcing his first wife.

My mother was the workhorse of our family. As a small child, she had seen the effects of the war, hiding guns, and my grandmother's reactions when the violence reached their doorstep. I believe that by the time she married my father, she had already trained herself well to block out bad things, to separate the good from the bad and cut the mental connection between the two. She was a survivor. Unfortunately, that meant that when my father was verbally and physically abusive to us, she simply became unresponsive until his temper cooled again, letting his words and blows roll off of her, focusing on the positive. And, after every bout of abuse, he'd turn around and act loving and affectionate.

As I've grown up, I have come to believe that my mom did the best she could with what she had while she was raising me. She did try to take care of me doing things like making my clothes all through my younger years, even sewing costumes for things like Halloween. She just wasn't mentally or emotionally present when bad verbal and physical things were happening. Psychologists call it a defense mechanism, and I can understand that desire to block out everything negative. Blocking it out makes it feel less real, and that's just how she survived.

Some of my earliest memories of my father were of him telling me that I was worthless, useless, and would never amount to anything. My mother always showed me love, but she rarely interfered when my dad was verbally abusing me. To this day, I believe that half the things I've done in my life was to prove him wrong.

I was a precocious five-year-old, so much so that I came home from my first day of kindergarten at the Greek Orthodox private school in Jamaica, Queens and told my mother, "I don't want to be there. All they're doing is coloring and not learning anything. This is a waste of time!" My mother called the principal and requested that I start first grade immediately, which of course I did!

Another memory of mine from younger days is my mom often telling me to play with Vincent or Anthony—kids I did NOT want to play with. I also remember a family that lived in an apartment above my parent's place that would watch me sometimes when I was four/five years old. Although my parents were beginning to make good money, we still lived in a less desirable part of town while they were building their dream properties.

The family living upstairs consisted of Nana and Joan, and her two daughters, Dawn and Cheryl, along with a little boy that wasn't all there mentally—his name escapes me to this day. It was an incredibly dysfunctional family. All Nana wanted to do was watch *Guiding Light,*and she would let me run around doing pretty much whatever I wanted to do. Even though Dawn and Cheryl taught me how to blow bubbles with bubble gum, they did drugs sometimes. Not the best environment for a child. The house I lived in was next to an expressway and one day Dawn and Cheryl got high and brought me down to the bridge over the expressway and dangled me over it from my ankles and threatened to drop me into oncoming traffic. Many years later I mentioned this memory to my mother, and she said she recalled hearing about that, but again, I was fine. I was alive so it was "okay."

One of the few times I remember my mom being there to do something for me as a kid was when she took me to the first McDonald's that opened in our area. I remember waiting two hours to see Ronald McDonald. These kid-like occurrences felt abnormal. My childhood was filled with very adult experiences. This would lead to me really wanting my kids to feel like they had a real *childhood,* whereas I was always left to fend for myself.

My mom used to take me to the Farmer's Market where she had a snack stand, and even there, vendor would watch me. I was always dumped on somebody to raise me. My parents felt like that since I was with an adult that I was fine. In my mind, being watched by everybody but my parents left me to feel as though everyone was my parent.

By my first year of grade school, my parents were doing well financially. They owned multiple restaurants, a yacht, properties, and a half-million dollar home on a private island.

I do have memories of fun things from back then though. For instance, I was very crafty when I was little, I found myself practicing needlepoint and crochet. My mom's restaurant was below the Sears and Macy's offices. I used to be their little model girl for when they'd do store window displays. I would make halter dresses and miniskirts for all of my Barbies from last year's samples from their books. I felt quite special since I was the only child ever in these corporate offices helping out at the time. I loved helping them with their displays. It's no wonder that Macy's is still my favorite store to this day.

At the age of seven, in 1969, I became the first child ever to travel alone on a transatlantic airplane. I take this as an early sign that I was destined to be in the travel business. My parents sent me by myself to visit family I'd never met in Greece for the summer. So, I took off on a hot, muggy July day on Air France with hardly any idea of what these family members looked like. I knew I was to stay with my aunt and my cousins, but that was all I was told. My aunt, a tall, robust woman, met me at the airport and took me home with her.

It's important to note that in 1969, Greece was in a period of political upheaval. The Junta had taken over the government, America was actively trying to establish a more diplomatic government, and we'd hear reports on the news of politically-motivated terrorism – like the series of bombings in Psihiko targeting US military vehicles, the US embassy, and US military officials. We lived under a lot of restrictions and rules, though I was too young for them to impact me much. At age seven, it didn't occur to me to mind that the Junta had banned the Beatles, Mark Twain, free press, labor unions, long hair on men, or the peace movement. I did mind, however, that none of the neighborhood kids wanted to play with me since I was American.

My aunt, Vangelio, worked as an embroiderer, designing and crafting children's crib sheets and wedding linens. In a day, she might stitch the entire story of the Three Little Pigs for a baby boy, or sprays of delicate

flowers for newlyweds. One day, she took me and one of my cousins with her to buy patterns in Salonica, the second-largest city in Greece. I remember running up and down the spiral stairs of the pattern store, playing hide-and-go-seek with my cousin until she yelled at us. "Stop it! Come here and stand by me!" Parents act like parents everywhere I guess.

The pattern department was on the seventh floor, but thankfully there was an elevator.It was a tiny, wooden closet-sized space with a large mirror at the back. We walked in, and my aunt moved straight back to

the mirror, facing the door. We huddled together in the back to admit more passengers when a group of foreigners crowded in, and kept cramming ever more tightly. My aunt tried to tell them "No! No! No! Too much weight!" in Greek, and I tried to tell them in English that she wanted them out, but either they didn't understand or wouldn't listen. My aunt wrapped both of her arms around us, covering us with her body, and was murmuring prayers when we felt the elevator drop out from under us.

We fell three floors. Then the elevator stopped with a bounce, before crashing through the final four floors. I remember blood everywhere, and bodies. Red, sticky, metallic-smelling blood gushed out of my aunt's arm which had been cut severely by the broken glass of the mirror behind us, that dangled at her side. She was still holding us close to her, covering our faces, trying to block out the horror of the scene when the first responders came. They pulled the bodies out one by one and sat my aunt down on the floor. They poured orange soda over her arm, tied a tourniquet around it and told her that no ambulance would come – she'd have to get herself to the hospital.

My cousin and I didn't have a scratch on us. Believe it or not, I don't remember any fear from that experience. I remember it like it was yesterday, and I recall being completely calm the entire time. My aunt had shielded us from both the impact and the glass. We walked with her, practically running, through the streets for blocks to reach the hospital. The nurses took her into a back room, and my cousin and I sat holding on to each other's hands tightly, waiting.

No one sent word back to my parents of what happened at first. Back then we didn't have cell phones and certainly didn't have social media. Still, eventually my parents heard about the accident, but they never came to my rescue. I know I wasn't hurt physically, but the fact that even my mother didn't even fly out to Greece to make sure I was okay was emotionally crippling. I always wondered how she could have left me there without coming to get me, as had it been my own children I would have hopped on a plane immediately to come to their aid. Then again, looking back—maybe she did try, but my overly possessive and controlling biological father might not have let her. Honestly, I wouldn't be surprised if that was the case.

I feel like something happened to me the day the elevator crashed, spiritually and emotionally. It was the first time I really understood that we have very little control over what happens to us, and the best you can do is to go with your gut. I believe in God, I believe in family, I believe in me, and I believe we're all here for a reason. And I go with that.

Here is the letter I've kept all these years telling my mom not to worry, but to this day I feel like she should have gotten on a plane to at least be by my side.

Greece 7/7/69

Part 1

Dear Mother and Father part 1
I came to Greese good they
piked me up from the areport
Gus piked me up from the
arcport and Mareanthy and
Xrestos the night time about
ten-ocklock we went to a Hote
the next day we were at
thesaloneke I sat in Raggolitin
one weke because there was
Ouranea and Stabros and we
could play together Satuday
Gus piket me up from
Raggeletsa because we had
to go some pl to swim
lemoo on the street Gus
put me on adonky and made
me a farmer and I went on
a horse and Gus mademe a pich
from Tammy Kavourakis

Part 2

Dont wore mom, erry
one is with me and
erry one loves me.

I kiss erry one
From Tammy,
Kavourakis

When I made it back home to the states, life went on as usual. From about seven and ten years old, my parents worked in their restaurants from early morning to late at night. Instead of returning to our empty house after school, I would walk one block down to my grandparents' house every day. Back then, I was very independent, and I guess you could say that would set the stage for the independence I have felt all of my life. All the vegetable stand owners knew me. I'd go to the pizzeria for a quarter and chat with the owner and waitresses and make regular rounds for the school fundraiser selling "World Famous Chocolates" at the used car lot next door. I remember the price was $0.35 cents a bar, and I found it funny that I knew *exactly* who to market to, car salesmen and their customers, while other kids were going door to door. I would not have to work as hard and still I would make the most sales!

As I said, I was very independent, and one thing I would frequently do was walk three miles, roughly 60 blocks, to see my only friend at the time – Pauline. It may be hard to believe that a girl in third and fourth grade would walk that far to see a friend, but this was the norm for me. After we finished playing I would then walk the 3 miles back before my parents ever got home. Pauline would later move down to Florida, and because we made a pact as children, she ultimately became Katie's godmother.

I was the neighborhood kid that everyone knew. Granted, this was before the days you had to constantly fear that a child would be kidnapped by a crazy pedophile, but it still is shocking to me just how free I was to wander about all the time.

Like many children of affluent families in our Greek neighborhood, I attended Greek school at St. Demetrios Greek Orthodox Church. There were twenty-five of us, and once we were ensconced in our seats, we were rarely allowed to move from them. Teachers were very strict. Every morning, I remember putting my hands out on the desk in front of me so my teacher could inspect the state of my nails. Too long, or dirty, and we'd feel the sharp sting of a ruler across our knuckles. We weren't even allowed to go to the bathroom unless it was during an officially sanctioned break, which inspired me to purposefully pee in my seat many times. I still remember the first time I did this; the stream spread halfway through the classroom while all the kids around me cringed away from the growing puddle, laughing. I sat there, stoic, defiant, and nervous, staring the teacher down. I got into big trouble when I was sent home early. My parents were not sympathetic to my act of rebellion.

I walked by myself to the bus stop each morning. Bored by classes that were going too slowly for me and teased relentlessly by the other kids, I was miserable. Even though she was busy, my mother made lunch for me every night to take to school with me the next morning. I was mostly self-sufficient by the age of five and got myself ready for school every morning, wash my face, brush my teeth, dress myself, pack my school bag, and make breakfast. I could make oatmeal, boiled eggs, and my father even taught me how to make poached eggs. Drizzling olive oil or butter onto his poached eggs, he would then sprinkle them with lemon, salt and pepper, and then top them with crumbled bread to soak up the egg yolk. To this day, I'd rather have a poached egg prepared that way than anything else. Then, before stepping out the door to go alone to the bus, I would grab mother's brown bagged lunch that she had made for me.

You know, you would think that since my parents owned multiple restaurants that my mother would have sent me to school with delicious Greek food or at least maybe a normal sandwich, but no. Unless there were leftovers, she would usually wrap an unopened can of tuna fish, half a lemon wedge, and a can opener in a brown paper bag. As I stood by the sink at school, draining the oil out of the can, the other kids would tease me about these odd lunches as they ate their chicken salad and turkey sandwiches. When mother felt inspired, she would make a white bread, cream cheese, and tomato sandwich – which I thought was horrible. I think these lunches are probably part of why I taught myself how to cook at a very young age. I will say this though; looking back at my meals over all as a child, I didn't eat much processed or fast food, and to this day I still don't.

St. Demetrius' student body was made up, almost exclusively, of Greek kids from the wealthiest families in the neighborhood, and they knew it. I never felt comfortable around them, certainly not accepted by them; so I went my own way, often spending lunchtimes with the lunch lady or the janitor. I would do things to deliberately provoke people, like wearing boots with my school uniform. If you saw a class photo, I would be the kid in boots, with the teacher's arm snaked around my shoulders, so she could dig her claws into me to keep me from talking.

One morning, I was so late for school that I'd missed the bus, and it was pouring rain outside. If I didn't get to school, I knew I'd be beaten when I got home. I couldn't walk to the school which was two miles away with my broken umbrella and tiny raincoat, so I broke open my piggy bank with a knife and hailed a cab. Picture that for a moment! A young child hailing a cab.

I snuck into the school lunch room, boots squelching with every step, and the lunch lady helped me dry off. Then, I ran down the halls to sneak into class, and smacked right into the principal, Mr. Kazepis. Mr. Kazepis was a small man, but a mean one. I think now that beating small children must have made him feel bigger somehow. But when I hurdled into him in that hallway, I knew I was in trouble. He began interrogating me with, "How did you get here?!" When I replied that I'd taken a cab, he slapped me with a backhand that started well behind his back for the windup. He marched me into his office and called my parents at their restaurant to come pick me up. Once at home, my father beat me for missing a day of school and interrupting their work day.

One of my most vivid childhood memories begins when my mother and I were walking down the beach on a brisk February morning and saw seagulls making their nests in the sand. The birds didn't appreciate us getting so close (in fact, there was a "Warning: Seagull Nesting Site" sign that we saw later), and began dive-bombing us by the dozens. I screamed, absolutely terrified of the attacking birds, and I was so mad at them that I took two eggs and put them in my coat pocket. The next Monday, at school, I wore the jacket with the eggs still inside. As usual, I folded it and placed it on the classroom heater to dry. Later that day, I came inside and found something peeping out of my jacket. One of the eggs was hatching! I hadn't thought of the egg as a real animal, and suddenly, there was a new baby seagull. I was so excited and brought the tiny bird to my teacher, believing she would know how to help it. The teacher took my seagull, looked at it, and crushed its neck with two fingers. I screamed "I hate you!" Her only reply was "It wasn't going to live anyway." I had nightmares for weeks after that. In the space of a few moments, I had something bad, made it into something good, and had it all taken away. It's a pattern that would repeat itself several times in my life.

- - -

When I was just turning ten, in 1971, we moved to Indian Bluff Island in Palm Harbor, Florida, which was four miles from Tarpon Springs, a Greek community closely connected with the community we'd left in New York. We lived in a large, 4,000 square foot house – one of only 70 homes on the island - with a pool that was built for parties. My parents had a vibrant social life, always hosting parties with signature dishes, like Shrimp Saganaki, and lots of booze. My father loved birds and built an aviary in back. On weekends, he taught me how to trap finches and parakeets to add to his collection. My parents had just opened up a new restaurant called Dunedin Grill, and I began work bussing tables. It was a happy time for me, at least for a little while.

Actually, here's a funny story from my days of bussing tables: I never spent all the tips I earned. I would walk the money over to the bank and deposit it. Years later I don't know where that money is, but I do vividly recall depositing it into a bank across the street because I wasn't taught to frivolously spend. I was taught to save.

My life had never been better. I rode my bike around the neighborhood, took piano lessons, babysat for the neighbors, and went to a school that couldn't have been more different than the rigid private Greek school I'd left in New York.

For the first time, I had some *real* freedom and I loved it. Eisenhower Elementary in Clearwater had an innovative program that gave each child all the work they had to do for the entire year at once, an experimental model that allowed students to work at their own pace. Used to the strict, regimented schedule of St. Demetrius, I thought this must be some kind of trick and that I'd get in trouble if I didn't finish the work fast. With this motivation, completing the year's worth of assignments took me three months, earning straight A's, and I spent the rest of the year painfully bored. The one thing that always upset me was that on award days I never received a single award. Even with my exemplary marks, my speed in learning and completing assignments, I was NEVER given the recognition I felt I deserved. This frustration would later lead me to aspire to as many awards in business as I could possibly achieve.

As a result of not having anything else to do because I finished my assignments so quickly, I landed in the principal's office frequently for having a bad attitude. My worst class was gym. I was too short to clear the hurdles on the school track, but Mrs. Heck (you never forget the names of some teachers, do you?), forced me over them anyway. I would fall flat on my face every time.

With my new found free time, I worked as a TA during school then walked to my parents' restaurant to buss tables. I also got involved with the local Greek Orthodox Church. I had an incredibly busy schedule, but that suited me fine.

In April of 1972, we took a vacation back to New York to visit my grandmother and our old friends, and see the sights like tourists do. One of my best friends was Angela, who had lived next door to me, so one evening I walked over to visit her. At my knock, her father opened the door. He was usually a friendly Italian, greeting everyone with a hug, a kiss, and a warm hello, but that night he was very cold. Aloof. Still, he invited me to join them for dinner, but something felt off. Besides, I had plans to see the new musical *Grease* at the Eden Theater that night with Pauline and her sister Kate. I said I'd come back to see Angela the next day.

Later that night when I returned from the theater, I saw the street filled with police cars and ambulances, the frenetic pulse of red and blue lights bouncing off the brick of Angela's house. My mother tried to lead me inside, telling me not to look, but I snuck out the back door to investigate anyway. I furtively ran over to the basement window and peered in, immediately wishing I hadn't. I saw blood everywhere, and body parts. Later, I learned that Angela's father had flown into a rage at dinner that night because there was no bread on the table. He killed his wife and butchered the bodies of everyone in the house with a hatchet. Ever since that horrific scene, I can't bring myself to watch horror movies because they are far too real for me.

Back in Palm Harbor, I kept up with school during the day, and bussing tables in the afternoon and evening; but even my busy schedule couldn't distract me from my parents' disintegrating marriage, which was getting worse by the day. Still, they kept up a solid family front for the neighbors, managing their restaurant, attending church, and hosting parties as always.

During one backyard barbeque in 1974, I splashed in the pool with ten other neighborhood kids, we heard a woman screaming. Curious to see what was happening, I jumped out of the pool, flung a towel over my shoulders and ran barefoot to the front yard, the other kids not far behind. We ran down the street with our towels, finding the woman ten homes down on the left. Leoda Jean Brownell was holding her throat, pink foam coming from her mouth and blood seeping through her fingers. A few yards further down the street was a man with a shotgun, and there was a dead leopard sprawled between them. The adults came, some staying with the injured woman, others ushering us kids back to the yard, hastily assuring us that she would be fine, but I knew she wouldn't be.

My parents would later tell me that the adults had spent precious minutes that could have been used to get her to the hospital faster arguing with the ambulance service about which ambulance was allowed to come and save this woman since we were on the island, outside their normal jurisdiction. By the time an ambulance finally arrived, sirens echoing through the neighborhood, she had stopped moving. I thought for sure I had just watched someone die, and that experience stuck with me after that.

Later, I learned one of our neighbors had been keeping this leopard in his garage as a pet, and Leoda has been feeding chickens to the big cat while he was away. The man with the shotgun was a hunter, and upon seeing the leopard's jaw clenched around her neck, he shot the leopard expertly, right between its two yellow eyes. Though he had shot the leopard to get it to let go of the woman, and she ultimately survived, that ridiculous argument could have left her for dead. It was that argument over the ambulance that lead me to question things, go against the grain, and become a strong debater.

- - -

The Leopard Attacked, Then

By FRANCES BRUSH

Of The Times Staff

CLEARWATER — Leoda Jean Brownell, the young Largo woman who was attacked by a friend's pet leopard at Indian Bluff Island last January, continues to recuperate at home from her injuries.

And she looks upon the incident, in which she nearly died, as a religious experience.

Mrs. Brownell's voice is still not quite right, and she says there is a numbness on the right side of her face. Still, she sees a blessing in her recovery.

the animal attacked her when she tried to throw a chicken to it in the garage.

SHE SAID she respected the animal enough to use care in opening the connecting door between the kitchen and the garage but the leopard shoved the door open, lunged at her throat, sinking its teeth in her neck and they both went down on the floor.

Mrs. Brownell paused to explain her religious feelings,. her deep faith in God. She said that when she was attacked she grabbed the gold cross she was wearing on a chain around her neck and began praising God.

said, and she did. With the leopard keeping its hold on her neck she managed to get out of the house where island residents saw her as she collapsed on the ground.

"It was my faith, but somebody one else coming to the rescue. Each one of those people who helped had a specific job to perform and they performed just as they were supposed to — the woman who screamed, the man who had the gun . . ."

IT WAS WHEN she heard the woman scream that she passed out because she knew then someone would help her, Jean Brownell says.

years old and a registered nurse, is that she continued her hold on the cross at her neck, yet when she got to the hospital the cross was in her clutched hand. When a nurse removed it from her neck the clasp was still closed, she says.

When she was admitted to the hospital after surgery she was not to be allowed to have visitors for two weeks because of the seriousness of her injuries.

In less time than that, 10 days actually, she was discharged.

THE NIGHT BEFORE the attack, Mrs. Brownell said,

about reaching night I prayed me to show peo the next day t she said.

Jean Browne with the frien when it was sn bitten her then.

Asked her op keeping wild an she says only p training and handling wild have them. She to see anything

Mrs. Brown her husband, a plegic veteran War, at 13677 Largo.

24

As I got older the physical, emotional, and mental abuse from my biological father continued to escalate. I think it was his own guilt in his mind that made him scarier. For example, everyone in school was going on trips, and he would say I couldn't go because I would get raped. He became very possessive over me and my mom. We weren't allowed to do anything or go anywhere because of him. He was so controlling and incredibly jealous of my mother doing anything for anyone but him. For example, I remember one instance where my mom wanted to buy my grandmother a heater and he wouldn't let her. My grandparents' heater had broken and my mom wanted to get them a portable heater to keep warm. They got into a massive argument that ended with him not allowing her to get a heater. It's not like my parents were hurting for money, and helping my grandparents wouldn't have hurt him at all. My mom just wanted to take care of family, but he wouldn't budge.

What was most irritating is he would be cheap about these kinds of things that could actually help others, but then he would splurge on nonsense for himself. The more I witnessed his selfishness and inability to take care of anyone other than himself, the less I wanted to be like him in every possible way.

By Junior High, my parents were going through a divorce, and by freshman year, my mother and I were essentially homeless and without income since everything we owned had been in my father's name – the restaurant, the house, the car. He would have taken me as well if he could have.

Before the divorce proceedings began, my parents went on one final vacation with me in a last ditch effort to save the marriage. I was between 10 and 12 and they rented a motor home to drive for three months through the United States. We went to every state in the United States with the exception of Alaska and Hawaii. They fought EVERY. SINGLE. DAY. It got so bad that one day while we were in Ruby Falls, my mom and I fled the motor home on foot. We were hitchhiking to get away from him. I'll never forget this.

The man that I'm embarrassed to call my biological father was, and still is, a complete psycho. He would later end up serving a prison sentence for raping my three-year old step-niece. After my parents divorced, I made it my mission to completely separate myself from him. I wanted nothing to do with him, and hoped I never see him again.

Once the divorce was finalized, my mother had a little money set aside, and one day she picked me up from school and asked, "Should we go to Greece for three months for vacation?" She had a piece of property on the water across from the house, and she could sell the property and save the money to get an apartment, or we could go to Greece. We chose Greece and had the best three months of our lives! We needed that time together and my mom needed that break. I'm so glad we went on that trip.

When we came back to the United States, I went to live with my grandmother who had moved to Tarpon Springs to be near us after my grandfather passed. My mother joined her new beau, Spiro Skordilis, in traveling around the country. He was also a famous Greek musician, and would soon become my stepfather.

- - -

I had three rules for myself in high school: no dating, no kissing, no fucking. I didn't have sex with anyone in my high school. I met my first boyfriend at Epiphany in January 1977, but he didn't go to my school. He went to Clearwater Central Catholic. He would ultimately be the one I lost my virginity to, but in high school our relationship wasn't about sex. We waited more than a year before we did the deed because unlike many of the girls in my school, I wanted it to mean something. I wanted it to be more than just a passing fling for my first time. We were young and not meant to last forever, but to this day we still communicate. I was driven, independent, and to my teachers, a total pain in the ass. One of my teachers wrote in my yearbook, "To the one student who kept me busy and honest all these years." I had caught another teacher smoking weed in the back of the school grounds with some of the kids, and had told the principal, but she didn't believe me. It had made me so angry that I slammed her glass door, sending shards flying everywhere. Many years later, I bumped into my old principal, and she told me she believed everything I'd ever told her, but couldn't do anything about it.

I was no angel as a teenager—I was very rebellious. Left totally unsupervised by my poor grandmother, I did whatever I wanted, including making fake ID's (using the Yellow Pages and a lamination machine) for my friends, talking back to teachers, wearing tube tops to school, drinking, smoking, partying, getting into fights, but mostly working. My goal was to make enough money to move back to New York as soon as possible, so every minute I wasn't in school, I had not just one job, but three jobs. I even went to junior college while I was in high school.

What most people don't know is the reason I was acting out was about more than just getting attention. I was depressed from the divorce of my mother and father. Up to this point, divorce wasn't a thing. None of my friends had divorced parents. In high school, I had another brush with death when I took what must have been 20 pain pills in a suicide attempt. My friend, Evan Psomas, found me and called for help, and this has been a secret between my friend Evan, my mother, and me until this book. I ended up in a coma for two days and then in therapy for a short stint after the fact. I also had a bout with pneumonia that rendered me hospitalized too. All of the stuff I was dealing with only pushed me harder to make my goal of getting to New York a reality after high school.

From age 14 to 16, I worked nights in my mother's restaurant, Evelyn's Shrimp boat, took classes at St. Pete Community College, and worked for Panama Jack's tanning oil company on Clearwater Beach as a squirt girl. I'd walk up and down the beach, from sunbather to sunbather, and spray people with tanning oil while wearing my bikini. The job often included wet T-shirt contests too – hey, I'll do anything to sell a product. Another unique part-time job I had was helping to keep mental patients clean at the infamous Anclote Manor Mental Institution, which was just down the street from my house, from 4 p.m. to 8 p.m. five days a week. It was just as creepy as it sounds. Interestingly enough, it used to be Al Capone's summer home.

I'd kept up with extracurricular activities too as statistician for the basketball team, the football team, and the wrestling team. And, as a member and original founder of the color guard of Tarpon High and Flag Girl, I had the guys all over me. I loved to flirt, and if any of the cute guys on the teams wanted to go over their stats, I always made time. One basketball player, Wayne Cooper, who is now a pastor in Los Angeles, turned pro after high school and told me once that knowing his stats had helped him a lot in college. I was happy to help. Below is a newspaper clipping photo and the passage that went along with it when I received my first award for community service involvement in 1989.

"Ever wonder what happened to that friendly, energetic girl who was statistician for Sponger Basketball and Wrestling teams and founded the school's Color Guard in the late 1970's? Tammy Kavourakis graduated in 1979 at 16 and moved to New York to work in an uncle's typesetting company. During her junior and senior years at Tarpon, she also took courses at St. Petersburg Junior College and worked at Anclote Manor, as well as her parents' restaurant, The Shrimp Boat." – *Tarpon Springs High School "Where Are They Now" 10 Year Reunion Flyer, 1989*

Since I had been moved up a grade in elementary school and took community college classes while in high school I graduated at 16. In typical rebel fashion, I was wearing a silver plastic bikini under my graduation gown and flashed everyone as soon as the ceremony ended.

Two weeks later, I packed up my duffel bag with clothes, threw it in the car, and drove to New York.

- - -

When you have so many tragic events happen in your childhood, you cope with the memories in one of two ways. One way is to spend hundreds of hours of your adult life on a psychologist's couch, read self-help books, and try to mend what's been broken by focusing on the past. That was never my way. I choose to live very much in the present, not ignoring the past, but not dwelling on it either. I don't mean to imply that this is in any way the healthier option, but I have found that when you stop living in the past, the past can become a powerful driving force that thrusts you into a fast-paced life of achievement. After all, when you stop looking back, you only have one option left: looking forward.

PART 2: NEW YORK WINS AND LOSSES

When I arrived in New York, I had a rough plan. I'd move in with my uncle and work for his typesetting business, but within a few weeks, I began to have this funny feeling that I was being watched and I thought I was being followed on the street. It was 1979, the Cold War was heating up and my uncle was a card-carrying member of the Labor Party. It quickly became apparent that my funny feeling wasn't so funny. My coworker, Andrea, had also begun to feel uncomfortably under surveillance, so we agreed to find an apartment together well away from Cold War spy games. After weeks of searching newspaper advertisements and hand-scrawled ads tacked up at the Laundromat, we finally found a place within our budget – in East Orange, New Jersey.

Back then, East Orange was a notoriously bad neighborhood – a real "'hood". Predominantly black, we could feel the racial tension the moment we stepped out of our place, but the rent was only two-hundred dollars a month, for which we shared an entire house with four people we'd never met. It was like MTV's *Real World* for sure. For the first few days, we thought we had really made it in the city. Then, after multiple threats on our lives from our neighbors, we decided it best to give up the house and go our separate ways. I moved in with my half-brother for a short time, moved about 10 more times between various places. Then, finally, found my very own tiny one-bedroom apartment in the much more affluent enclave of Riverdale, New York City.

Known for its turn-of-the-century mansions built by Manhattan's early moguls, Riverdale couldn't have been more different than East Orange, and I felt like I had finally found my place in New York City. And I was determined to make a success of it. To pay my rent, I lied about my age (still 17) and worked at three diners as hostess and waitress: the Broadway Diner during the day, the Georgia Diner at night, and Tiffany's in Manhattan in the morning. On December 1st, 1980, I handed in my notice at two of the diners and traded them for a job working as a secretary at Adam International shipping company on Broadway, just up the road from the World Trade Center.

Adam International sold 220 volt appliances wholesale to the Mediterranean – mostly to Greece, Sudan, Haiti and the Middle East. The family-run business needed a secretary who could also act as translator, which meant my Greek upbringing was a significant resume enhancement.

I wrote letters, typed, assisted with whatever was needed, but I was given strict instructions not to speak to anyone or sell anything. After work, I would grab dinner on the way back to my apartment in Riverdale where I would catch a quick nap, and change into my hostess uniform for the late shift at the Broadway Diner from 8pm to 2am. During the day, I would flirt with my manager, the store owner's son; at night, I had a much less welcome admirer—Nick Artemiades. Nick was a server at the diner who came up to me at the same time every night and asked the same question, "Will you go out with me?" I told him that I didn't go out with anyone, which was true at the time. While I wasn't opposed to enjoying the 1980s nightlife New York had to offer, I wasn't interested in dating. I was too busy being a responsible adult with my own jobs, my own car payments, and pursuing my goal to save up enough money to open my own business. I was so busy taking charge of my life at 17 that I hardly even spoke to my family, although I did keep in touch with letters (I didn't have a phone from 1979 until 1981) and an occasional call. I kept saying no to Nick, and he just kept on asking.

Over the next six months, my job at Adam International went very well. I'd earned a raise with my promotion to a sales position, and was looking forward to finally leaving the night shift at the diner. My life in New York was finally starting to take off, and I was already making connections and developing partnerships to advance my career goals.

Between jobs, my studio apartment was my sanctuary, a symbol of my independence that I cherished. Located within easy walking distance of Van Cordland Park in the Bronx, and just a few minutes' drive from downtown, it had everything a girl could want, including a small kitchen with bi-fold doors that would open accordion-style for use, and close for company,. There was enough room for a bed, a small table with two chairs, and a piano that my parents had bought for me at a young age from when I used to take singing and piano lessons. For "safety" bars had been soldered onto all the windows by the fire escape.

Early one morning after finishing another late shift, I came into my apartment and promptly crashed. Later that night I woke up feeling heat. I was hot and sweaty and felt like I was engulfed in flames. Sure enough, all over my sanctuary were large flames blackening my refrigerator, flickering through the accordion doors, and nearly engulfing my piano. With bars on the window, my only choice was to run out the way I'd come in, so I crawled out my front door and began frantically knocking on all the doors down the hall to warn my neighbors of the fire. Finally, one of the other tenants came out with a growling dog and a baseball bat, but once he saw what was happening, he helped me get the people out of the building.

Once the firefighters had left and the police came, the investigation found proof of arson. It quickly came out that Nick had followed me to my apartment, and told the the landlord, "My ex-wife has all of my stuff in her apartment and won't give it back. Can you let me in for five minutes? That's it, and I'll leave. You know what it's like, she's my ex..." Almost true to his word, it only took him five minutes to roll up newspapers and stuff them inside the coils of my old refrigerator, where they were sure to catch fire during the night – and could have burned me alive in my sleep.

It was a long night. I salvaged a few smoky clothes, and anything else that hadn't been completely burnt, and stored them in my car overnight while I stayed in one of my neighbor's apartments. The next morning when I walked out to the street where my car was parked to drive to work, it was gone. Someone had seen all of my belongings inside and had stolen it. Days later the police found it at La Guardia airport. In the space of two days, I'd lost everything. I nearly lost my job at Adam International too, because when I told my boss what had happened, he basically didn't believe me. Luckily, he finally came around, and I was able to keep the job.

They never caught Nick, but a few years later, my husband and I walked into a restaurant in New York, sat down in our booth, and when I looked up I recognized our server: Nick. Before we could react, he briskly walked away and disappeared.

Here are a couple of letters that I wrote home to my mom in August 1979 while I was in New York on my own, my mom kept them all of these years:

Oh yea I got your card tha nk-you and I'm very
lucky to have you as my mother. What other mother
lets his or her daughter leave on their own at 16?
I ll tell you one thing... when people tell you
its rough out there its really not I'ss just how
rough you want to make bt on yourself. Anyone can
find h is happiness right in foont of him. The more
he searches the less he finds. Mom I really hope
you get out of Florida and move to New York.

Hi mom,

How are you doing? I'm ok I guess, we
had this terrible thing happen
in our building at work. As you can
see the newspaper clippings. Two
weeks before the murder this woman
had gotten mugged and raped on
our bathroom. They don't think that
it was the same guy because the
first guy had a gun and this guy
had a knife. Anyway ... we're all
under tight security and we've
been using the mens bathroom.
Sheing, saw the whole thing
from beginning to end, his going
through this temporary thing.
you know now I don't want
to scare you or anything but it
could of been me. I missed the
killing by 5 minutes, on the same
floor and everything. But I'm
lucky, Mom so that's enough
of that ugly news. whats new
with you? I'm ok, I guess,

37

My manager at Adam International, Sherif Yuksel, was ten years older than I was and handsome. He was also the owner's nephew and a notorious playboy. When we met, he was dating four other women, but the charms of a flirtatious 17-year-old, (posing as eighteen – I lied about my age on the application), were difficult to resist. By the Fourth of July in 1981, I had whittled his list of ladies down to one, and our relationship literally began with fireworks. At work though, we were strictly business, knowing his uncle wouldn't approve of an office romance.

In the entire time I worked for Adam International, I only took time off twice: once for the fire, and once on a day with such heavy rainfall that no customer was likely to brave the flood. Our building was very old, with an aged ambience I can only describe as Perry Mason. Before I left for the day, I walked up from our 8th floor office to the ladies room on the 9th floor to take care of business. On my way out of the bathroom, I bumped into the wife of one of the clerks, gave a brief greeting, and went on my way.

That evening, Sherif called me with news I had to sit down to hear. Minutes after I'd left, Sherif heard screams from the bathroom and ran in to find the clerk's wife bleeding on the floor from multiple stab wounds. He pulled her limp body to the elevator for safety and called the police. Later, we learned the missing pieces of the story, that the stabber had been recently released from prison, for good behavior no less, and had hidden in a bathroom stall in the ladies room, planning to rob the next person who came in. When the clerk's wife resisted, he stabbed her. I was very much aware that, but for a matter of minutes, it could have been me. Below is the clipping I have kept after all these years:

A mother stabbed to death — ex-con is nabbed

By PHILIP MESSING

AN EX-CON who served 10 years for homicide was arrested again yesterday for allegedly ambushing a Queens mother in an office rest room and stabbing her to death with a butcher knife.

According to police, Olga Rodriguez, 42, a mother of three children, was stabbed under the left breast by Milton Silim Jones, 39.

Mrs. Rodriguez' husband, John, 52, was slashed in the face, arms and hands when he tried to come to her assistance, said police.

He was taken to Beekman Downtown Hospital where he was treated and released.

The tragedy came only hours before the pair were to leave on a business-pleasure trip to Puerto Rico, police said.

The incident occurred at about 5:15 p.m. when Mrs. Rodriguez, co-owner of Mar Forwarding Limited, a freight-shipping firm at 198 Broadway, left her eighth-floor office to go to a washroom on the ninth floor.

Moments later, in an apparent robbery attempt, Jones pounced on the woman and stabbed her to death, authorities said.

Alerted by her screams, Rodriguez ran up the stairwell and confronted the assailant with a second man who had run down from the 11th floor.

Desperate to escape, Jones allegedly flailed out at Rodriguez — slashing him and nicking an unidentified bystander.

Jones, of 1313 Amsterdam Av., was arrested shortly afterward and charged with Mrs. Rodriguez' murder.

A source said Jones was released from Greenhaven Correctional Facility under the state's "good-time" law on Feb. 23, 1986 after serving 10 years on a 5-to-15 year sentence for homicide.

The Rodriguez home is at 89-61 212th Pl., Jamaica, Queens. They have two sons and a daughter, aged 5 to 17.

Woman Is Slain in Office Building; Husband Is Hurt Subduing Suspect

By JOSH BARBANEL

A 40-year-old woman was stabbed to death last night in a bathroom on the ninth floor of an office building in lower Manhattan, the police said. Moments later, her husband received head cuts as he and two other men subdued a suspect.

The police theorized that the suspect either attacked the woman during a robbery attempt or was surprised by her as he hid in the bathroom in preparation for a burglary in the building later.

The dead woman, Olga Rodriguez, and her husband, Juan, operated a freight-forwarding business, Jar Forwarding, on the eighth floor of the building, at 198 Broadway. According to the police, Mrs. Rodriguez was stabbed in the heart at 5:15 P.M. as she entered a women's room on the ninth floor that is normally kept locked.

Found on Stairway

As Mrs. Rodriguez stumbled into the hallway and onto the stairwell, her husband and several of his employees heard her screams and ran to her aid. Mr. Rodriguez was cut as they struggled to subdue a man they found on the stairway between the eighth and ninth floors.

"When the police arrived, one of the employees was sitting on him, and another was wrestling the knife away," said Sgt. Donald Disken of the First Precinct detectives.

The suspect, 29-year-old Milton Salin Jones of 1313 Amsterdam Avenue was arrested and charged with homicide and possession of a dangerous weapon. Ser-

geant Disken said detectives were looking into a possible link to other robberies in Lower Manhattan office buildings.

Mr. Rodriguez was treated at Beekman Downtown Hospital and released.

Sergeant Disken said the Rodriguezes ran an apparently prosperous worldwide business. The office is in a narrow 12-story building, two blocks south of City Hall, with a camera store on the ground floor and small employment agencies, law, insurance and accounting offices on the floors above.

The Rodriguezes lived in a one-family frame house at 89-61 212th Place in Queens Village, and had three children — two sons, 8 and 18 years old, and a 4-year-old daughter.

"They were wonderful, happy people," just hard-working people," said one neighbor, Carmen Herrera.

After more than a year of working for Adam International, I knew enough about the business to realize that Sherif's uncle wasn't making as much money as he could. Each wholesale 220 volt appliance order we sold had to be purchased by us and then shipped onto the client via a middle man. As the assistant, I had spent the better part of the previous year making arrangements with our shippers to export appliances, which had given me an idea.

One day, I called the owner of our usual shipping company and laid out my plan. I said, "The way it works now, the client comes to us first to buy appliances, and then we ship them through you, which means you're only making maybe twenty-percent on the deal. I think we could both make more money if we formed one company that can sell and ship wholesale. I get 30% of the shipping, you get 30% of the appliance sales, we work together, and I want to be a partner." I can only imagine what that middle-aged man must have thought during the long pause that followed my speech, but in the end, the numbers made sense. We struck the deal and this became my first strategic partnership, and would set the stage for my future as an entrepreneur.

Sherif and I, now nineteen, forged a new company with the shipping business and called it Marathon International, part of 7 Islands Packing Express: a full-service appliance wholesale and shipping company specializing in the Mediterranean region. Sherif proposed, but I had one hesitation. The idea of having the name "Tammy Yuksel" wasn't doing it for me. I bluntly told him, "I'm not Yuk-anything. Change your name, or no dice." Sherif's actual first name was Levent, so we changed his first name to his last name, and I became Tammy Levent. Shortly after that on June 6, 1982, Sherif and I were married and were promptly fired from Adam International upon returning from our weekend honeymoon on the Jersey Shore.

Our wedding marked the beginning of one of the most exciting and successful periods of my life. It felt like we could do anything. Thanks to the strategic partnership I'd formed, our export business took off from the very beginning, leveraging contacts we already had and quickly forming new ones. Throughout the rest of the 1980s, we were the top company for export shipping to the Mediterranean in the United States. By the time I turned twenty, we were making millions.

- - -

In 1982, Sherif and I moved to New Jersey where we concentrated on building our business and making money. We expanded the business to shipping furniture, boats, and other very large cargo, and I loved every minute of it. One of our regular customers was a man named Eddie Argitakos, an accountant from Queens. A few months after I first saw him come in, I opened up the newspaper and was shocked to see his face on the cover. Eddie Argitakos had been arrested for the largest cash heist in U.S. history — and some of the eleven-million dollars was never found. Personally, I think we might have shipped it to Greece without ever knowing!

By 1984, our business was starting to lose money. Open trade had started in Europe, which meant that shipping everything from the U.S. was no longer necessary. We became so poor that a meal of New Jersey beefsteak, tomatoes, and cheese and crackers was more frequent than I care to remember. We always had wine though, because Sherif took a part time job at a wine shop. We commuted to our jobs two hours each way to save on rent, but as the business began losing more and more money, it became clear it was time for something new. I often wrote home to my mother so that she would not worry about me, and so that I could vent some of my frustrations to someone who I knew would understand. Below is a small clipping of a letter from 1981.

I welcomed the change because I had just found out that I was finally pregnant. I wanted to move back to Florida to be near my mother and grandmother, and Sherif reluctantly agreed. However, having to run our business meant that much of the move was left up to others. My mother and grandmother scouted the neighborhoods around Tarpon Springs and found one they said was perfect. Although we hadn't seen it, they seemed positive that this was the place, so we gave them the go-ahead to make the purchase.

So, in July of 1985, pregnant and emotional, I walked into my first house for the first time. It was trashed. The kitchen hadn't been updated since the 1950s, and everything needed to be cleaned. I sat down and cried.

But, my mother and grandmother helped me scrub every inch of the place. We painted, picked out new furniture, and I fell in love with the 1950s oven. Even though I've since renovated the house extensively, that oven remains in my kitchen and is my favorite part of the house. For 30 years, I've cooked my mother's and grandmother's recipes on that stove for friends and family, and it is still in pristine condition.

In the first few days of September 1985 during Labor Day weekend, Hurricane Elena hit the Gulf Coast of Florida, blowing into a Category Three hurricane that would produce the largest peacetime evacuation the United States had ever seen. In the midst of gale force winds, I was experiencing my own tropical depression. Six months pregnant and dehydrated, I was feeling so bad that Sherif had to drive me to the hospital with rain pounding against our car at fifty miles per hour, and wind rocking our car from side to side on the slick highways. As we entered the hospital, doctors and nurses were already preparing patients for evacuation, but in the midst of the madness, I was in Tampa General and they delivered the news that my pregnancy was in trouble. My body had gone into pre-term labor. The doctors ordered me to stay in bed through the rest of my pregnancy and we went home.

Hundreds of homes were destroyed in Florida that fall, but for the next two and a half months, I could only watch from the sidelines since I was on bed rest to save the baby. To pass the time I obsessed over my new business idea: jewelry. Our shipping business had continued to lose clients, and I was determined to invest in a new venture that would give me more flexibility with the new baby.

In March of 1986, my daughter Katie was born, and I was finally allowed out of bed – though with the sleepless nights of early parenthood, all I wanted to do was crawl back in. I'd had so much downtime to plan my next steps though that it didn't take me long to begin networking. Little Katie was the best salesperson anyone could ask for. I'd take her into hair salons and boutiques, baby in one hand, a case of jewelry in the other, and ask the owners to sell my jewelry in their stores. In two years, I built up enough demand and inventory for us to open up our own store, right next to our Shop N' Ship location in Palm Harbor. We called it Park Avenue Jewelers, Inc., and its first official day of business was Halloween, October 31st of 1987.

The opening of this store marked my second strategic partnership. Here's how it came about. When Katie was a baby, I was going through a Burger King drive through and saw that Shop N' Ship at Alderman and US 19 was for sale. I was wearing little blue shorts, flip flops and a little white shirt with baby throw up all over me. I walked in and asked for the landlord. The receptionist was of course sizing me up at that point. Who goes into an office dressed liked this asking for the owner? Me, apparently!

I said I wanted to meet the landlord and learned it was Chuck Gorrow. I looked at him and told him I needed to rent some space to open a jewelry store.

Chuck asked, "Do you have any money?"

I said, "No."

Then he asked, "Do you have any collateral?"

I said, "No."

Chuck asked, "Can you get a bank loan?"

I said, "No," and then offered an alternative: Instead of taking a loan or offering collateral, I would take over the Shop N' Ship store and run it for him and that I just need about $100,000 to make this work. Then, I looked him straight in his eyes and asked, "Would you give me the money?"

He said, "I don't know anybody in the world who would have just met me, come in here and say to me give me $100,000." He then said, "Because you have balls and because you walked in here and asked this I'm going to give it to you. It's clear you have no fear and I think you will make this work."

For the first five years of Katie's life, we ran both businesses at the same time. Like my parents as I was growing up, Sherif and I were very active entrepreneurs, leaving Katie in the loving and capable hands of her grandmother and great grandmother much of the time. We expanded Shop N' Ship into a packing, shipping, giftware, international appliance and electronics retailer, and adapted to the changing market by using shipping containers to relocate entire households from the U.S. to the Mediterranean. With the vibrant community of Tarpon Springs nearby, we did a brisk trade, even while the Gulf War was backing up the overseas shipping schedule. Sherif handled the physical labor, along with our crew, and I was in charge of everything else. I sold appliances, filled out the paperwork, coordinated forklifts, trucks, trains, and ships, and did a lot of trouble-shooting. The crew called me the "pit bull" – I think it was a compliment.

On a typical day, we might load a forty-foot container with the belongings of twelve families – everything from a grandfather clock, to dishes, to a new car. In fact, one of the more memorable items we were asked to ship was a $38,000 chandelier that was seven feet tall and five feed wide from Natchez, Mississippi to Mytilene, a little town on Lesbos Island in the Aegean Sea. Since the chandelier had to be hung the entire time to ensure none of its crystals broke or its metal bent under its weight, Sherif had the idea to hang it from the ceiling of the shipping container, bracing the bottom with tires, and tying the entire thing with a web of ropes to keep it immobile on the six-thousand mile journey. One of our crew members quipped that we packed that chandelier like it was nitroglycerine. It arrived without a scratch.

One of the more challenging questions we had was how to ship a small boat on a trailer that was four inches too tall to fit in the container. This reminds me of the riddle: "How do you get a tall truck through a tunnel that's one-inch too short?" We suggested we deflate the tires. Between selling 220-volt appliances, (cheaper to buy here and ship to Greece than to buy there), trouble-shooting the odd requests, and running the jewelry store, Sherif and I were stretched almost beyond what we could bear. Still with our entrepreneur mindsets, neither one of us could see any other option. It meant, however, that Katie and Jordan – our son born in 1992 – spent much of their young lives with their grandmother, just as I had.

On the next two pages, you will see a clipping from the local newspapers about us and our business:

Shipping business all in the family

■ A couple makes a life of shipping families' belongings to Greece.

By CRAIG PITTMAN
Times Staff Writer

Times photo — JACK ROWLAND

The crew loads a car into a truck. The contents of an entire house can be squeezed into a 40-foot shipping container.

PALM HARBOR — Outside the boxy steel container, there's a cool breeze. Inside it's hot as an oven. The men work quickly, carrying in wooden crates and steamer trunks and stacking them up to the ceiling.

In two hours they've loaded the 40-foot container with the belongings of 12 families, everything from a grandfather clock to a new car, all bound for Greece.

Heading the four-man crew is Sherif Levent, 38. Levent and his wife, Tammy, 28, own Shop N Ship, a business on Alt. U.S. 19 in Palm Harbor that sells appliances to people moving to Europe and ships their household goods across the ocean.

"We pack everything — dishes, furniture, pictures, rugs — anything," Levent said. "With the exception of personal undergarments."

About 40 percent of their business comes from middle-age Greek couples leaving Tarpon Springs for their homeland.

"Usually they're in their 40s or 50s," Mrs. Levent said. "They say they're going down there for good, but they end up having a home there and a home here."

The rest of the Levents' business comes from Greek families scattered around the South. Once the crew went to Natchez, Miss., to move a Greek family to the island of Mitilini. Their belongings included a $38,000 chandelier that was 7 feet tall and 5 feet across — much too large for a packing crate.

The crew hung it from the ceiling of the container, braced the bottom with tires and tied it down with a web of ropes.

"We packed that chandelier like you pack nitroglycerin," said crew member Michael Salvi, 54.

The chandelier made it to Greece intact. But Levent says the Mississippi-to-Mitilini move marks the only time he broke anything. When he arrived in Natchez to give the family a price estimate, he opened their front door too fast and smashed a lamp.

Levent handles the physical end of the business. His wife sells the appliances, fills out the paper work and coordinates the forklifts, trucks, trains and ships that carry the goods.

Levent's crew calls her "a pit bull."

Love came later

Tammy Kavourkis was just 16 when she graduated from Tarpon Springs High in 1979. A week later, she moved to New York City to work for her uncle's typesetting company.

The following year she met the man she would marry, a Turk named Levent who ran an export business and was looking for a secretary who spoke Greek.

"She ruined life for me," Levent said with a smile. "I was dating four different girls at the time."

The teen-ager lied about her age and typing skills and landed the job. Then she set about landing the boss. She couldn't type, but she could do something else.

"She was a very good cook," Levent said. "That was it. Love came later."

Levent converted to the Greek Orthodox faith and they married in 1982

Please see SHIPPING Page 2

48

Shipping from Page 1

and moved to Florida. Now they have a 5-year-old daughter named Katie who says she's ready to take over when mom retires.

Mom will be a tough act to follow. One moment she's explaining, in English, how the Persian Gulf war has backed up the overseas shipping schedule. The next minute she's talking in Greek to a man who wants to ship a motor home that's 4 inches too big to fit in the container.

"If he deflates the tires he can get another 2 inches," she said.

She knows

Sherif Levent doesn't have to explain his day when he gets home.

When families move overseas, Mrs. Levent shows them a catalog of appliances they can order for their new home. Unlike American goods, which work on 110-volt current, these refrigerators and washers will work on the 220-volt current common to Europe.

As the appliances arrive, the Levents store them until there are enough to fill a container. Then the crew packs everything up, building the crates themselves.

Two weeks ago a trucker arrived at a Holiday warehouse pulling an empty 40-foot container, ready for Levent's multinational crew: Salvi, who's Italian, Jimmy Vanvoris, 24, who's Korean, and Dimitri Kostakis, 25, who's Greek.

After they stacked all the crates in the container, they nailed up a plywood wall to keep them from shifting. The hammering echoed in the steel container like a string of firecrackers going off in a coffee can.

Once the wall was up, Levent cranked up a Honda and drove it up onto the flat bed of a big tow truck Mrs. Levent ordered from Clearwater. The tow truck backed up to the container, Levent backed the car in and Salvi and Kostakis chained down the wheels. Then they repeated the procedure with a brand new Toyota.

Levent noted the irony of buying Japanese cars in America and shipping them to Greece, but said it makes sense. "Cars are cheaper to buy here," he said.

To ship a full load costs about $7,000, although that can vary depending on the size and type of items. The contents of a typical three-bedroom house would

Times photo — JIM DAMASKE

Tammy Levent handles shipping arrangements for the business.

fit in one 40-foot container and weigh about 32,000 pounds, said Mrs. Levent.

Sometimes the crew packs a container so full that Levent has to push the doors shut with a forklift. This time, there was plenty of room to close the doors.

The truck pulled out and headed for the railroad, where the container would be loaded onto a train bound for Savannah, Ga. In Savannah, a crane would put it on a freighter bound for Piraeus, where in 28 to 45 days the cars, the clock and everything else would be claimed by the owners.

A sweating Levent swigged some Gatorade and regarded the end of a day's labor and the advantage of being in business with his wife.

"I would hate to have to go home at the end of a long day and explain what I did all day," Levent said.

"This way, she knows."

49

PART 3: LOSING EVERYTHING, THE SECOND TIME

For five years, we worked and saved and finally made the jewelry store lucrative enough to allow us to sell Shop N' Ship to just concentrate on one business venture instead of two. Jordan was born in January of 1992, and he was an energetic baby determined to be the center of attention – a Kavourakis family characteristic, I suspect.

That year on Halloween night, the fifth anniversary of opening Park Avenue Jewelers, I hauled Jordan, dressed as a corn on the cob, and Katie, flouncing in a princess dress, to her school for their annual Halloween Parade. As the little ghosts, witches, princesses, and superheroes marched, my nerves were becoming increasingly frayed. Little Jordan was not amused by the noise or the corn costume and fussed loudly in protest; and while juggling him in one hand, I was fielding a series of beeps and buzzes from my pager (this was before cell phones). I finally excused myself and left early to go home and call the store to check on Sherif because I had a bad feeling.

When I ultimately reached the store, Sherif was in the ambulance and he was unrecognizable. At the hospital, what little of him I could see between bandages and casts was bruised and cut. Sherif had a black eye, a torn ear, and his jaw had been knocked out of alignment – these were the most visible injuries. The doctor walked into the room and told me in a low voice that my husband had sustained between fifty and sixty blows to the head and was dealing with brain damage.

Earlier that day, Sherif and one employee had been working behind the counter when two men walked in. The first man was over six feet tall and a solid two-hundred pounds, while the other man was slim and carried a briefcase. While they came in together, they acted as if they didn't know each other. The larger man approached the counter, pulled out a pendant with a diamond in the center, and asked Sherif about putting in a larger stone, and while they were discussing the possibilities, the man with the briefcase interrupted to ask about a special kind of chain—which we didn't carry. The two men left and Sherif thought nothing of it.

Around 11 a.m., Marietta, our employee went to lunch and Sherif was alone in the store. The large man returned with the pendant and asked what it would look like if he added two more diamonds, and as Sherif turned around to show him with the cubic zirconia we kept in the store, the man leaned across the counter and punched him. Sherif crumpled to the floor as the man with the briefcase walked in, and together the two men jumped on top of him, kicking and punching him, while trying to bind him with duct tape.

When you're being beaten, getting knocked out is a blessing. But Sherif, hard-headed Turk that he was, wouldn't go out. Sherif used to box back in Turkey, and his father was a five-star general in the Turkish Army, which I believe explains the fifty to sixty punches to the face. Between blows, he told them he'd be quiet and begged them to stop hitting. The men demanded diamonds, but we didn't carry any. Then they asked if we had money in the safe – we didn't. The larger man sat on top of Sherif behind the counter while his partner cleaned out all of the jewelry on display, nearly our entire inventory. The door opened, and Sherif heard the man with the briefcase say, "Ma'am, we're closed." The customer left hurriedly. The distraction was just enough for Sherif to work a hand free and get to his feet. They hadn't shown him a gun or a knife yet, so he thought he could resist and traded a few punches with his captors. It didn't take them long though to push him into the wall, one holding him there while the other grabbed his neck to choke him. They threw him on the floor, and he heard one of them say, "This is it. You're going to die now."

As Sherif took what he thought was his last breath, he heard the bells on the door jingle again as another customer entered. This customer realized something was wrong, shouting "Hey!" and the robbers ran out, punching the unfortunate customer and shoving two others out of the way. They drove off in a stolen Lincoln. Here are two clippings about the incident that almost cost Sherif his life:

Anything but happy anniversary

■ Sherif and Tammy Levent say they will reopen their 5-year-old jewelry store after a robbery in which he was badly beaten. They just don't know with what.

By CRAIG PITTMAN
Times Staff Writer

PALM HARBOR — Some anniversary.

Five years to the day after he opened his jewelry store at Alt. U.S. 19 and Alderman Road, Sherif Levent stood amid empty display cases Saturday and tried to tear a sandwich into pieces small enough to eat.

He was having trouble chewing because he couldn't bite down. Two men robbed Park Avenue Jewelers on Friday, and they beat Levent so severely that they tore his ear, blackened his eye and knocked his jaw out of alignment.

Then, Levent said, one robber told the other one, "We have to kill him."

"I kind of took a last breath," said Levent,

39. "I kind of let myself go, getting ready to die."

Just then, though, a customer walked in, and the two robbers fled. In their briefcase, they carried thousands of dollars worth of jewelry — and Levent's hopes for the future.

"We lost everything we had worked for," he said. "Everything we had was in our inventory."

Levent and his wife, Tammy, 29, started their business with $1,500 in borrowed cash, and built it up to the point where Levent figures their inventory totaled more than $65,000. He estimates the robbers took 95 percent of that.

Levent had no insurance on the business. The premiums cost too much for a small store to pay and still keep prices competitive, he said.

When the two men first entered the jewelry store Friday morning, Levent and one employee were working behind the counter. He thought the men were customers.

The first man was 6 feet 2 and weighed

Times photo — SCOTT KEELER
Sherif Levent of Park Avenue Jewelers stands by an empty display case.

Please see **ANNIVERSARY** Page 3

Anniversary
from Page 1

perhaps 200 pounds, Levent said. The second one, who was slimmer, carried a briefcase, he said. The two did not act as if they knew each other.

The first one showed Levent a pendant with a diamond in the center, and talked to him about putting in a larger stone. The one with the briefcase interrupted them to ask about a special type of chain, which Levent told him the store did not carry. The slimmer man left, and the one with the pendant left after a while as well.

About 2 p.m., Levent's employee left the store. So Levent was alone when the man with the pendant returned and asked what it would look like if he added two more diamonds.

Levent said he could show him with cubic zirconia, and turned to get them as the man with the briefcase walked in. Then the man with the pendant leaned across the counter.

"He out of nowhere sucker-punched me," Levent said. "I fell."

The two jumped on top of Levent, rolled him over onto his face and tried to bind him with duct tape, meanwhile kicking and punching him.

"They were trying to knock me out, but I wouldn't go out," Levent said. "I told them I was going to be quiet, and not to hit me."

The men demanded diamonds, but Levent said he didn't have any

> **Sherif Levent and his wife, Tammy, started their business with $1,500 in borrowed cash, and built it up to the point where Levent figures their inventory totaled more than $65,000.**

on the premises. They asked if the safe held any money and Levent said no.

The man with the briefcase began cleaning out the jewelry on display, while the larger man sat on top of Levent. Then Levent heard the door open.

The man sitting on Levent laid down flat behind the counter, so he couldn't be seen, and the man with the briefcase said, "Ma'am, we're closed." The customer left and the robbery continued.

By then, though, Levent had managed to work one hand free, and he jumped to his feet. "We started exchanging punches," he said.

He hoped to make enough noise to attract attention, but that was impossible. The two stores on either side of Park Avenue are empty, and no one heard the struggle.

"They pushed me toward the

wall and one of them grabbed me around the neck and started choking me," Levent said. "Then they put me back down on the floor. Up until then, they hadn't shown me a gun or a knife so I thought I could resist. I felt strong enough."

But as the robbers pushed his face into the floor again, he heard one of them say: "This is it. You're going to die now."

"When I heard that," Levent said, "for the first time I got scared."

At that moment, though, the door opened again — more customers. Levent heard one of them say, "Hey!"

"That's what saved me," Levent said.

The robbers jumped up and ran out, punching one of the customers and shoving the others out of the way. They drove off in a champagne-colored Lincoln with a stolen Palm Beach license plate. Some people in the parking lot tried to chase them, but lost the car on the highway, Mrs. Levent said.

Saturday afternoon, a battered Levent wiped away tears and said he does not know what he will do now. He's hoping that the customers who saw the robbers — the woman who walked in and left, and the others who accidentally saved his life — will get in touch with the Sheriff's Office.

He said he expects to reopen for business Wednesday — but with what, he wasn't sure.

"We're not going to close," Mrs. Levent promised. "We're going to figure something out."

Sherif kept his life, but we lost everything else that day. Our entire stock had been on display, which we had bought with borrowed money and had left uninsured; the premiums cost too much for us to pay and keep prices competitive. We owed our jewelry wholesalers $65,000, and our other creditors even more, including our mortgage company. With his head injury and substantial emotional trauma, Sherif wasn't able to work, which meant that I needed to make money as soon as possible – in any way possible.

Chuck Gorrow was so kind to me after the robbery. We still owed him about $15,000 but he wrote off the debt because he said he made enough in interest back. Fast forward many years, and I learned Chuck died and I decided to go to the funeral. I saw his wife Patti and she told me that even though they used to have a lot of money, he died with a lot of debt and she said, "I need money." So now, two decades later Patti is working for me. You don't throw people away! Build relationships because you never know where you will end up and who you may need some day.

- - -

With medical bills, debt, a mortgage to pay, and two children to feed and clothe, we needed income right away. So, I took the first job that hired me: a scam telemarketing company called Vacation Break. "Congratulations! You've won a trip to the Bahamas! And it's a timeshare property." Yes, I was the woman who scammed your parents into floating on a timeshare boat for four days in the Bahamas.

I could sell ice to an Eskimo, let me tell you. Not only would I get Granny on the phone, I'd make each deal sound so promising that she'd have to tell her sisters, friends, cousins, children, and grandchildren about it. Each call I made resulted in multiple sales. But, I wasn't getting rewarded for my hard work, so when the chance came to jump ship to another telemarketing company, I took it.

Sky International was a lofty name for a room with twenty people in it. But, it was a growing company, and grew even faster as I made telemarketing calls that resulted in multiple sales. This time though, my efforts were noticed, and I was promoted to writing sales scripts and training new employees. The trick to telemarketing is to sound like a real human being and find common ground with the person on the other end of the line - fast. Once you establish that human connection, making the sale is easy. However, if you sound like you're rattling off a call center script, they'll hang up.

So, I became "Tammy the Trainer" in an office rife with nicknames. Our boss, Cheryl Weiss Mercuris, was "the little general," and like Napoleon, she ordered people around and spread fear of her throughout the office. She and I had many run-ins when I thought she'd stepped over the line with an employee under my tutelage, and she probably would have fired me if I weren't so valuable to her company. But, I loved my trainees.

On April 10, 1995, when I was promoted my trainees presented me with the gag gift of a small whip, and afterward whenever I was training a new recruit over the phone, I'd have that whip in my hand and play with it. I'd practice using the whip to flip paperclips into a cup, which required focus, and more than a little coordination. It was a small, silly thing, but at that time in my life when I felt completely out of control, holding that whip made me feel powerful. My marriage was eroding, I rarely saw my children because my work hours were so long, and I knew that my company made its money through scamming people. In that situation, finding that you have control over something as small as flipping paperclips becomes significant. It's easy to feel like your circumstances define you, but the truth I found – through flipping paperclips – is that I had the power to control my future. Slowly, I started to form a plan, but I was in no financial position to do anything but keep working.

For over two years, I worked twelve to 14 hour days, seven days a week. Sherif's physical and mental recovery meant that he couldn't work for a long time, but eventually he found a job selling cars. With stress over money and overwork, we were fighting more and more. While my grandmother took excellent care of my children, I missed being there for them in the mornings and evenings. During this sad time, I'd go to work before they woke up and I'd return just as they were going to bed. I barely had time to ask them how their days had gone.

On a warm spring afternoon April 11, 1995, as I was sitting at my desk, alternately staring at the waving palm trees in the parking lot and drilling telemarketing wisdom into the head of a new recruit, two policemen walked into the office and asked for me. They said there had been a car accident with my grandmother and my children. As usual, my grandmother was driving Jordan and Katie to her house less than a mile away, after school. Along the way, my 79-year-old grandmother passed out at the wheel. A large green power truck was driving into her lane and she passed out from fear. Katie, seeing that YiaYia had passed out, tried to take control of the car and put it in park, but she didn't know how, and the car crashed into the front steps of a house on Bayshore Drive. My YiaYia died on impact and Katie, who was nine at the time, and Jordan, three, were critically injured.

Katie couldn't remember any of this for the longest time, and the papers reported that my YiaYia had a stroke at the wheel, but it wasn't what happened. Jordan remembers a cop was wearing a bandana and that he didn't want a stranger messing with him, but that's it. Many years later Katie realized that what caused the accident was that big green Florida power truck coming into the lane.

Here is a photo of my YiaYia's car after the accident, as well as a newspaper clipping about the accident that claimed her life and almost the lives of my children.

St. Petersburg Times
North Pinellas Times

NORTH PINELLAS EDITION — ST. PETERSBURG, FLA.

WEDNESDAY, APR. 12, 1995

Great-grandmother dies when car hits house

■ The woman's two great-grandchildren, ages 7 and 3, are injured in the accident.

By AMY WALSH
Times Staff Writer

TARPON SPRINGS — A 78-year-old woman with her two great-grandchildren in the car died Tuesday when

she lost control of the vehicle and it ran into the front steps of a newly rebuilt home.

Evelyn K. Kalimtgis of 1675 Seabreeze Drive likely suffered a heart attack or other medical problem before her 1993 white Ford Escort crashed, said Sgt. Ron Surmin of the Tarpon Springs Police Department.

He said there were no skid marks or any sign that the driver tried to avoid a collision.

She was pronounced dead in the driveway at 702 Bayshore Drive shortly after the accident, which occurred about 1:45 p.m., Surmin said.

Kalimtgis' great-grandchildren — Katie Levante, 7, and her brother Jordan, 3 — were admitted to All Children's Hospital in St. Petersburg. Katie was in guarded condition and Jordan in fair condition, a nursing supervisor said.

Kalimtgis was wearing a lap and

The 1993 Ford Escort driven by Evelyn K. Kalimtgis sits in front of the entry steps of a newly rebuilt home on Bayshore Drive.

Times photo — JOAN KADEL FENTON

Please see CAR Page 3

St. Petersburg Times

Amy Walsh

April 12, 1995

TARPON SPRINGS- A 78 year-old woman with her two great-grandchildren in the car died Tuesday when she lost control of the vehicle and it ran into the front steps of a newly rebuilt home.

Evelyn K. Kalimtgis of 1675 Seabreeze Drive likely suffered a heart attack or other medical problem before her 1993 white Ford Escort crashed, said Sgt. Ron Surmin of the Tarpon Springs Police Department.

Car From Page 1

shoulder seat belt. Police said they think Katie, who was in the front passenger seat, was wearing only a lap belt. Jordan was in the back seat. He was wearing no seat belt and was not in a car seat, police said.

Police speculated on the cause of the crash because no one saw it happen. "There are only witnesses to the sound of the crash," Surmin said.

The great-grandmother and children were traveling from the children's home on Park Avenue to the woman's home on Seabreeze Drive.

The car, its front end crumpled, its windshield shattered and its frame bent, came to rest in the carved driveway in front of the Assimack family home at 702 Bayshore.

Tire tracks were barely visible in the front lawn next door, showing the car's path through the grass, across the neighbor's driveway and the Assimacks' driveway and into the steps. In all, the car traveled about 150 feet after leaving the road.

A side-view mirror lay in the grass between the two driveways, where the car had missed a utility pole, but apparently brushed its guy wire. The Escort passed within inches of a fire hydrant in the neighbor's yard.

The accident Tuesday was the third calamity at the Assimack home, which sits on Kreamer Bayou. The neighborhood is in northwest Tarpon Springs on winding streets that hug the Anclote River and its tributaries.

An attic fire forced the family out in December 1992, and the house flooded during the no-name storm in March 1993, said Peter Assimack, who lives there with his parents.

The Assimacks razed the house that flooded and built a new two-story home on the site. They moved into the gleaming white home March 31. Assimack said he doesn't consider the house unlucky, but "maybe the location."

Assimack's father, Tommy, was the only person home when the car hit. He was upstairs listening to jazz when he heard the crash.

"I looked out the window and there was the car," said the elder Assimack.

His next-door neighbors also heard the crash and ran outside. The driver was unconscious and one child was screaming, said Julie Travers.

Casey Laspibar was the first to reach the car. He was installing sprinklers four houses to the south when he heard the impact.

Police could not say Tuesday how fast the car was traveling when it hit. An investigation is under way.

When Katie took the wheel and wrecked, the air conditioner went through the car and hit Katie in the face. The engine impacted and killed my YiaYia, but the air conditioner went through Katie's mouth. Jordan didn't have a seat belt on so he flew forward too, but he wasn't as badly injured as Katie was.

YiaYia with her beautiful flowers

58

Cheryl's husband, Kosta Mercuris, drove me to the hospital, where I learned that Katie needed surgery to have her tongue reattached.The the doctors weren't certain she'd be able to speak normally again. Jordan was also being carefully monitored, since a broken bone over his right eye was fragmented and the swelling was pushing bone shards towards his eye. The hospital feared Jordan would be blind because his optic nerve was pinched in the accident. They had to wait until the swelling went down before they could do the surgery to reconstruct his eye—taking a piece of rib bone to do this.

Katie was in complete shock. Jordan was more stable, but the doctors said Katie's tongue was cut off and down her throat. If she hadn't been as swollen as she was around her mouth, jaw, and head, she would have swallowed her tongue. Instead, she was incredibly lucky that it was

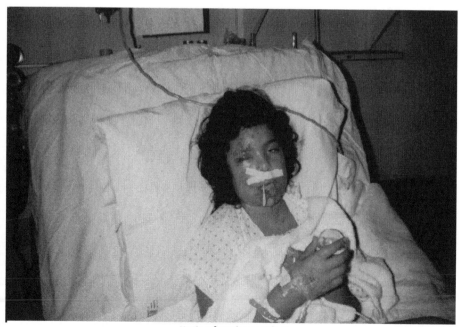

Katie after the accident

stuck in her throat because they were able to retrieve it and re-attach it.

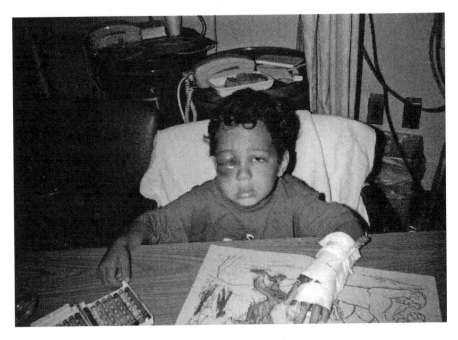

Jordan after the accident

For two days I sat at their bedsides in the ICU, nearly out of my mind with worry and grief. I was feeding Katie with an eye dropper because she didn't want a feeding tube. One day as I reached to give Katie her drinking straw, the hospital phone rang. When I answered Cheryl, the "little general," was on the line and had the audacity to ask, "So, when will you be back in the office? I need you to train."

Needless to say, my response of "%&#$ you" got me fired. The accident was Tuesday and she called me on Thursday. How could anyone be so heartless to expect you back to work so soon after a tragedy like this?

It's important to note that the accident happened during Holy Week and it just so happened I had the whip in my purse the whole time. While I was watching my children, images of Jesus along with other religious images for Easter were playing on the television. I just kept holding that whip because it was the only thing holding me together.

As I was watching this, I kept thinking of an acronym for whip: We Have Infinite Power. I'm watching my children, possibly dying in their hospital beds, we could get through this because we have infinite power.

To say the situation was grim would be a gross understatement. The

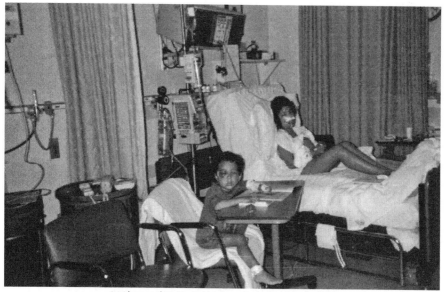

Jordan and Katie in the hospital after the accident

doctors and nurses were so concerned they even called a priest to come and sit with me. Low and behold, the man that walked into that hospital room was my childhood friend, George Patides. I went to school with him and he later became a priest. His father was in the band with my biological father. In the 1950s, George and I were practically in the crib together. I hadn't seen him for years. Then, all these years later, a St. Pete hospital calls in a priest to pray with me during Holy Week and it's George that walks in! I don't believe in coincidences.

George would later do my dad, Spiro's, eulogy and he will do mine if I die before he does. He and I are like brother and sister and I love him dearly.

Since the jewelry store robbery, I had been working desperately to pay down over $200,000 of debt from our failed business and keep our home. Now, with medical bills mounting from Katie and Jordan's treatment in intensive care, I was out of work and felt completely out of control. Once again, I had lost everything I'd worked to build, and at this point, I was exhausted. For the first time in my life, I didn't have my grandmother to help me through the pain—which made me feel her loss even more. She had such strength, had endured so much, and remained so kind. I couldn't ask for a better example to follow.

Katie and Jordan were in the hospital for weeks, and I became part of the hospital "family," chatting with the nurses as they came in and out. One day, I was especially tired from staying up half the night with worry, and when the nurse and I began chatting. I shared my concerns with her, told her that I didn't know what I was going to do. I explained how wasn't sure how I was going to pay for my children's care, or how I was going to keep a roof over our heads. I must have looked close to crying (again) when she paused and asked me a question I have never forgotten, "If it had nothing to do with money, what would you do?" I said the first response I that came into my mind, "I would travel the world."

- - -

She brought me the newspaper and I found a job working for the corporate travel agency, Aero Travel. I looked forward to the boss taking me under his wing, and I was determined to learn everything I could about corporate and incentive travel. My boss told me to go door to door and cold-pitch strangers on corporate incentives. This first piece of advice seemed to me a non-starter. Alarmed, I argued, "I'll never get anywhere in Tampa!"

Either his advice wasn't that bad after all, or someone up there was looking out for me, because the first corporate incentive account I landed was FritoLay—followed by PepsiCola. Just being myself, learning and reading a lot helped me along my way.

Within two years, I built up a loyal following of corporate and incentive travel clients. I was ready to grow. I wanted to expand into new markets, take on more clients, get a raise – and every idea I brought into the boss's office was shut down. Alas, my boss didn't want to grow or change. This frustrated me immensely.

It didn't take long for this frustration with Aero to build to a tipping point. I've never been one to sit still and my boss's lack of ambition was stifling. So, I called the top clients in my rolodex and told them I was forming my own company, "Elite Travel," and asked if they would come with me. FritoLay and PepsiCola both gave me an enthusiastic ,"Yes", along with several more of my favorite clients. I put down the phone, took a deep breath, stood up, and marched into my boss's office and quit.

It turned out that I quit just in time, since a few months later the federal government came and took his licenses since he hadn't paid taxes in a very long time.

One thing you need to know about me—I want the best, and I want to be the best. That is how I cobbled together the name of "Elite Travel". It was a reflection of my determination to be among the best in my business, but the name was incomplete. It was 1997, I was running Elite Travel out of my house for the first few months I wanted my company to sound like there was more than one person in it, so Elite Travel became "Elite Travel Management Group." I was determined to make this aspiration into reality as soon as possible, but I had no money, was still in $180,000 of debt, and the mounting medical bills from the kids' accident.

A few months after working my business from home, a friend of mine in Tarpon Springs asked me if I wanted to come to his office and work from there. I was there six months, and then left because I learned he was a crook and I just could not function that way. God must have been with me when I decided to leave because I went the next day to Eckerd drug store, opened up the *Tampa Bay Business Journal* (for the first time in my life) and there was a list of the top 25 travel agencies in the

Tampa Bay Area.

After looking over the list of agencies, I landed on what would become my third strategic partnership, Bay Travel, a woman owned agency. The owner's name was Brenda Allen and I called her up, told her I had loads of clients, but needed a business to work with. Within a week, I was in her office and had agreed to give them 30% of all of my sales to pay my rent, my employees, and allow us the use of their office.

During the years of trying to start and grow my business, my personal life had some bumps. Sherif and I had a pretty good life until the robbery. We were fine as a couple until he was beaten up that day. Afterward he was in complete denial. He definitely was suffering from Post-Traumatic Stress Disorder, had gotten violent, and just wasn't the same person any more. Then, the accident that nearly took my kids' lives happened and things just got worse. Living with Sherif wasn't safe for me or my kids anymore.

In 1998, I divorced Sherif and soon after was involved in a second hit and run accident of my own. The first hit and run happened to me just before I started at Bay Travel. I was sitting at a red light and saw a guy coming across the median right towards me. He hit me head on, then fled the scene leaving me severely injured and in need of shoulder surgery. The guy that hit me in the second accident was going about 90 and was drunk. After he hit me my car was totaled. I decided I was not going to let a second person get away with hitting me, hurting me and fleeing. So, I followed him back to his home and called the police after it happened. I suffered a ruptured disk from the second accident and had to have surgery on my neck. That was just the beginning. Not only was the surgeon who handled my neck surgery arrested two weeks later for doing cocaine while operating on me and several other patients—but while I was with Bay travel, I also had gallbladder surgery, a hysterectomy and a host of other health issues. It's like I had to rebuild my own body as I was trying to rebuild my life and build my still new company.

Also in 1998, corporate travel took a big swing – they took down our commissions, so Bay Travel began charging fees. Now, at this point I was engaged and I told my then fiancé that I needed to get into leisure and destination weddings because they would be the hottest trend. I don't really like to talk about it much because it was a short courtship and subsequent marriage based on delusions of grandeur, but significant things happened for me and my business during our time together nonetheless.

While I was at my final fitting for my wedding dress in April of 1998, the girl that was hemming my dress accidentally cut the hemline up instead of longer for the train. I had no dress at this point and my wedding was days away. I was devastated. It just so happened that there was a man in the bridal shop that day who owned a wedding magazine and was trying to make me feel better while he smoothed things over because this shop was one of his clients. After we got to talking about my travel business, he said he'd give me a free ad, a free booth at one of his shows, and put me on the front cover of a magazine too.

It should be noted that this man was one of the scummiest wedding people in the business—but free publicity, and an economy proof business like weddings and honeymoons sounded mighty appealing to me. Needless to say, I had my wedding dress within a week, we honeymooned in St. Lucia and I would come back to do the wedding show later.

- - -

In 1998, St. Lucia was off the radar for honeymoon locations. It would be years before Oprah Winfrey would name the island and its World Heritage Site one of the, "5 Places to See in Your Lifetime," driving business to its burgeoning tourism industry. But, when I visited the new Grande Lucian Sandals resort, the island had the feel of a place untouched by time – or tourism. I'm happy to say that it still does. Fast forward more than two decades, and I won the award for the 2014 Saint Lucia's Top Producing Travel Agents for the Piton Awards Program. I guess you could say my love for this place grew by leaps and bounds over the years, and I couldn't help but share this love with my clients who also fell in love with St. Lucia after they visited too.

- - -

I came back from my honeymoon and I knew I had to work on lead generation and put together a giveaway. I told my partners Don and Brenda Allen, who owned the travel agency, the whole story. Sure enough, the wedding magazine did put me on their cover as the owner of Elite Travel and gave me a booth at Harbor View bridal show. The day of the show, I did my first Sandals booking with Shane Fletcher, the first honeymoon I ever booked, and they went to St. Lucia. He actually ended up working for me in 2001 for a short period of time just before

9/11 happened.

In the next couple of years, I continued doing wedding shows and building myself up as *the* honeymoon and destination weddings expert of Tampa Bay. In 1999, my longest standing employee began working for me. Her name is Ruth. I put an ad in the paper and told her flat out that I had no money to pay her, but that she could work on a commission basis. I also told her that if she believed in my company, and in me, she would make good money. Judy followed in 2000 and my mom began working for me too.

I tell all of my employees up front that I will help them get leads and build their business, but they have to treat it as though it's their own business. That way they will get further ahead. It's all commission based, and they can choose whether or not they will come in. I can do the training and help them along the way, and even help them with new accounts, but in the end I believe it is up to each of my employees to make their own salaries. Now, 16 years later, Ruth is still working for me on commission only and she is still crushing it!

I knew that my company was on the rise, and wanted to take those who believed in my dreams for the future with me. Unfortunately, the partners I was working with did not seem to want to get into the wedding business with me. Don Allen was a very fair person, he gave me an opportunity and believed in me—which did a lot for my future, but he did not like change.

I knew it was time to move on. My contract with him and Brenda at Bay Travel stated that whatever I come with, I leave with, and I decided to tell him I was leaving. He told me I would never make it. I was with them until September 1, 2001 and in that time I grew to $4 million in traveled business in year one, and $8 million after that. After that four year stretch, corporate travel was declining and we were losing money so we went our separate ways.

AGENT LIFE
TRA

Walking down the aisle of success

Tammy Ehrhardt had been in outside sales working to build up another agency's leisure business before joining Clearwater, Fla.-based Bay Travel International in that capacity in 1997. Today she is national sales director of the company, which has a staff of 40 and close to $15 million in sales.

"I'm one who likes to go for the top," said Ehrhardt. "I want to be No. 1 and I have to surround myself with other high achievers."

She believes if agents focus on the sales and marketing sides of the business instead of just travel, they will be much more profitable.

Ehrhardt appears on ABC's 'Consumer Updates' to give away free honeymoons.

Ehrhardt worked hard to build Bay Travel's leisure division from nothing to 40% of the business. "I was working 15 hours a day, seven days a week trying to increase our leisure sales with virtually no staff," she recalled.

Realizing that approximately 20,000 brides were getting married in the Tampa Bay area yearly without travel professionals to assist them, she started a honeymoon division in the fall of 1998. In May 2000, she became a partner in the company, and opened her own leisure division in Clearwater, which became the company's headquarters.

From the beginning, the agency partnered with a local magazine, Tampa Bay's Best Wedding & Party Planner and became affiliated with The Perfect Wedding

Guide. In fact, she met the editor of the Wedding & Party Planner in a bridal shop for the final dress fitting before her own wedding. The editor wanted to feature her story and put Ehrhardt and her husband on the cover of the magazine.

After three months as a member of the Tampa Bay Bridal Association, Ehrhardt became its vice president and now appears on ABC's "Consumer Updates" to give away free honeymoons to unsuspecting brides and grooms.

The typical reaction Ehrhardt's prize patrol receives from winning brides.

"I've become known as the Santa Claus of the travel business," she said.

Ehrhardt attributes the agency's success and dramatic growth to lots of hard work and determination. "I have a drive to succeed and want us to do all we can to help the brides and leisure clients we work with," she said. She keeps her cellular phone on 24 hours a day in case of emergencies.

In addition, Bay Travel hires staff with personality and sales skills as opposed to travel experience. A year ago, she had just seven agents in the leisure division. Now there are 30, with four more on the way.

"I'm trying to hire two or three agents a week to keep up with all the business. I would like to have 100 agents by the end of the year," she said.

Ehrhardt added that many of her local independent contractors enjoy coming in to headquarters for the camaraderie and environment that exists.

BY MICHELE SAN FILIPPO

Ehrhardt, right, awards a free honeymoon to Couples' Swept Away resort in Negril, Jamaica.

Sweet rewards

Clearwater, Fla.-based Bay Travel has come up with several ways to reward its staff. The agency gives a free night's stay every time agents sell a package to a Sandals or Couples resort. It splits bonus commissions and pays agents 30% to 35% commission. When agents generate leads themselves, they earn 50% commission.

The agency also pays commissions when deposits are made, except for group travel. National sales director Tammy Ehrhardt added, "I'm taking a chance operating this way, but I've never been out of money yet."

She also doesn't believe in typical fam trips, but that agents should experience destinations as their clients would. Ruth Bowden, a Bay Travel agent for a year now, said she likes being able to "see and do" what she is selling.

"It was very scary becoming a commissioned agent, but now I'm making more money than ever and feel like my own boss," Bowden said.

Ehrhardt added, "I don't pressure [agents]. They want to do well because they are creating their own paychecks."

According to Bowden, "[Ehrhardt] is always giving out some kind of prize as an incentive each month for the person with the highest sales."

Ehrhardt explained that the more the agency sells, the more it receives from preferred vendors in terms of giveaways and fams.

Bay Travel sends direct mailings to about 35,000 brides a month, which represents the leads it obtains from bridal shows, magazine articles and the company's Web site, at www.honeymoongiveaway.com.

With Ehrhardt's incentives, her staff finds Bay Travel an ideal place to work. She's at the top in the photo above.

Executives at Bay Travel pride themselves on setting goals and achieving them.

"Satisfying customers has become an obsession. I want to be known for providing excellent service and establishing life-long relationships," Ehrhardt said. "My goal is to make their honeymoon the best trip ever so that clients return for all their vacation needs."

PART 4: MY KIDS – KATIE AND JORDAN

I wanted to take a break here for a moment from my story, and go a little deeper into the stories of my children as they were growing up. I've added bits and pieces of their lives throughout other parts of the book, and most of their stories will be for their own memoirs someday, should they ever choose to write them, but there is so much more I want to tell. So, I thought I would share what happened after the car accident that took my grandmother, and nearly took them, and where my kids are today.

After the car accident in 1995, my daughter Katie's face was severely cut up and her tongue was severed to the point that she couldn't talk. She was very scared, but she was, and is, a survivor like me. She was a dancer and a singer before the accident, but afterward had this severely cut leg and tongue, and nobody paid attention to her desire to sing because they treated her as a disabled child.

I recall just after the accident she wanted nothing more than to dance in her recital. The accident happened in April, the doctors said she might never walk again, but Katie insisted that she would dance in her recital in June. As a testament to her willpower, Katie gave it her all and sure enough danced in June in front of 2,000 people. There wasn't a dry eye in the room because everyone knew what she had been through.

Katie had a lot of visible damage. You wouldn't know that now looking at her, but every day was difficult repairing her skin after the accident until she was fully healed. Every four hours, I would have to take peroxide and water and clean the wounds. Then, I would peel all her scabs and put Neosporin on the wounds. The pain was excruciating and broke my heart, but without these treatments she would have ended up having reconstructive surgery, or who knows? We had to do this several months.

Katie had just turned 9 when the accident happened, and I was trying to rehabilitate her self-esteem and her body. Over the next five years, we worked to rehabilitate her and I even launched a record label to support her music. Katie quickly taught me that even if you have a handicap, you can overcome it.

Come the age of 12, I helped her create her first demo and by the age of 14, I was getting her singing gigs. I started strategically partnering to get her singing gigs. I convinced a program that was held at Tropicana Field in St. Pete, to let her sing. The organization was the Pinellas County Doorways Program which was a program for kids awarded scholarships that otherwise may not go to college. She performed at their annual celebration event. By this time, Katie was already performing in so many venues and we had met big musical acts like the Backstreet Boys. She even spoke to Howie D from the group, and he was the opening act for Katie to perform. It was incredible and the kids were so excited! It was suddenly all about promoting Katie. One company I partnered with was Evatone, and they helped me get Katie copies of her demo for free because of her story.

KATIE LEVENT

— Continued from page 18

performing but giving inspirational speeches to 9 and 10 year olds, teaching them to hold fast to their dreams. She has also established the Katie Levent Foundation, donating proceeds from her CD sales to numerous educational programs and scholarship funds across the country.

Katie Levent is a very special young lady, who was able to turn tragedy into triumph and claim her dreams over insurmountable odds. ❏

ENTERTAINMENT CONNECTION

A clipping about Katie and her singing

KATIE LEVENT

Turning Tragedy Into Triumph!

BY DONNA Y. CALDWELL

When Katie was only nine, she was in a horrific car accident. Doctors were doubtful that she would either walk or talk again, much less sing or dance...

Katie Levent was a born dancer. She was only 10 months old when she awed her family and a few hundred party-goers by stealing the stage to perform a really cute belly dance for the appreciative crowd. Her mom entered the talented tot in a beauty mother had a heart attack at the wheel, collapsed on Katie's lap and crashed the car into a house. Kate's great grandmother died and her three-year-old brother, who was in the back seat, broke a bone over his right eye. Katie lacerated her knee and nearly severed her of her songs was recently featured on the Lifetime television show, *The Division.*

As her career blossoms, Katie's experience has prompted her to view life from a unique vantage point. "I have

Another clipping about Katie and her singing

They gave us a total of 10,000 copies, and we sent 5,000 off to producers and people to try and get her a record deal. The other 5,000 went to kids for motivational purposes. Soon Katie was performing all over the country to spread a message of hope. She wasn't getting paid for her performances, but it wasn't about the money at this point. She had a message to deliver and everyone was helping her deliver that message.

One of her songs from her demo got played on a TV show, "The Division." It was a cop show being produced by Paramount, and it landed on the show thanks to Luke, a guy we knew that worked in television. It just so happened that Berry Gordy, founder of Motown, was working on this show and got wind of Katie's story and decided that

Teenager poised for singing stardom

■ Katie Levent and her mother have big plans. The 16-year-old Tarpon singer and belly dancer was chosen to perform at Music Fest Miami.

By TERRI D. REEVES
Times Correspondent

TARPON SPRINGS — Katie Levent was 9 when her great-grandmother passed out at the wheel of a car, collapsed on Katie's lap and pinned her to her seat. As Katie frantically tried to steer to safety, the car crashed into a house.

Katie's great-grandmother, 78-year-old Evelyn Kalintgis, died in the wreck, and Katie's 3-year-old brother, Jordan, broke a bone over his right eye. Katie's knee was lacerated. Her tongue was nearly severed.

"The doctors didn't know if she would be able to talk normally again," said her mother, Tammy Levent-Ehrhardt. Katie had to be fed with an eyedropper and faced months of physical therapy to learn to walk again.

Times photo — SCOTT KEELER

Katie Levent, 16, of Tarpon Springs is pursuing a professional singing career. As a grade-schooler, she was in a car accident in which her tongue was nearly severed.

Seven years later, Katie not only walks and talks, but sings and dances.

On Sunday, the 16-year-old Tarpon Springs resident was scheduled to perform on the main stage during Music Fest Miami, an all-day concert with entertainers such as Patti LaBelle and other local and international recording artists.

Katie submitted a demo CD to the festival committee and was one of 30 acts chosen to perform.

"I was very surprised that the committee chose me among the 65 (acts) that tried out," she said. "This will be one of my biggest performances yet and could lead to a big break for me."

Whether Katie reaches her goal of superstardom will be determined by the music-buying public. She knows achieving the goal will take hard work.

Please see **SINGER** Page 4

Katie should get the Unsung Hero Award— only a handful of kids have gotten this award. The Supremes presented the award to her and she got to meet them, Berry Gordy, Smokey Robinson, Stevie Wonder and so many other amazing artists. The following year they invited her to perform and give the Legends award to that year's winner, Tina Marie.

Katie was a performer, a dancer, a choreographer, and as much money as I could give went into her singing and dancing, because I wanted to prove to her that nothing was going to stop her. I guess Katie learned early on to adapt the attitude that both my grandmother and my mother had— that you can do anything, be anything, no matter what's happened to you in your past. I home schooled Katie in high school because she was called scar face by the kids. I wanted her to be able to focus as we worked on her act. From her sophomore to senior year, I ran my travel business and the record label simultaneously and we traveled all over for her performances.

On Labor Day weekend in 2002, Kate got to open for Pattie Labelle, one year I got to take Katie to the Grammys and eventually she would make in onto the show "America's Got Talent." However, the dream for her to become a world famous singer took a back seat. When she got to the age of 16, I was simply out of money. I'd invested more than $60,000 into her music, and with everything going on in my business, I had no more to give. Today, Katie is still doing various things in the music industry behind the scenes. She is writing music, doing covers, and helping her boyfriend produce in her spare time. She is also the Vice President of Elite Travel. I don't ever plan on retiring, but she is currently on track to take over the company after I'm gone.

Katie and Stevie Wonder

Singer from Page 1

and good fortune. But she hopes her Mediterranean-flavored rhythm and blues songs and unique blend of hip-hop and belly dancing will shake up the music world.

Her mother and manager — or "mommyger," as she calls herself — predicts it will.

"I really think there is a big interest in world music, and I think the Greek influence is going to be a part of that scene," Mrs. Levent-Ehrhardt said. "Look at the success of (the movie) *My Big Fat Greek Wedding*. There is another Greek movie coming out soon. And the fact that the 2004 Olympics are going to be held in Greece."

The 40-year-old mommyger not only believes it, she banks on it. In the past four months, she has put together a marketing package for Katie that includes professionally produced posters, media kits, videos and CDs.

She has hired big names in the business to work with her daughter: Tampa and Miami vocal coach Mary Walkley; music producer Ky Miller and entertainment attorney Matt Middleton, both of New York; and choreographer Geona Roberts, as well as four backup dancers, all from Orlando.

In addition, Mrs. Levent-Ehrhardt, who owns Elite Travel in Clearwater, used her connections to book Katie in venues in Jamaica and the Turks and Caicos Islands.

She won't say exactly how much she has spent on Katie's career but hints that in the past four months it is probably in the $35,000 to $40,000 range. That also includes travel, lodging, food and costumes for Katie and her dancers.

"To me, it's a business investment," Mrs. Levent-Ehrhardt says. "I built my agency to a $6-million-a-year business in four years. I feel that strongly about Katie and her talents. She has proven to me that she is committed and has what it takes. You do the most you can for your children. That, too, is part of the Greek culture."

At the tender age of 1, Katie made her first appearance in a beauty contest. She won the Miss Baby Tarpon Springs at 15 months with her belly dancing act, making her the youngest contestant to compete in the talent category. When she wasn't on stage, she gave impromptu performances for her family's houseguests.

During school, she entered many talent shows and joined the chorus.

She also spent a lot of time in her grandfather's studio, where he would play his bouzouki, a Greek guitar, and she would dance and sing. Spiro Skordilis, a 72-year-old native of Greece, had several hit records in that country. He plays the bouzouki on her CD.

Katie has also written some of her own songs.

"I write when the mood hits me," she said. One time she wrote a song in the middle of an exam, much to the chagrin of her teacher.

She attended Tarpon Springs High School her freshman and sophomore years, but is now home-schooled so she can devote more time to her career.

On Friday, though, she is scheduled to return to Tarpon Springs High to sing the national anthem at a football game. She will sell copies of her CD, with proceeds benefitting the students.

Katie hopes to attend the University of Miami, where she plans to major in international law or sports medicine. Her immediate goal is to sign a recording contract with a big studio, but if it does not happen, she says she can live with that.

"For me it's not about the fame or money," she said. "I just enjoy doing it."

Continued clippings about Katie

My beautiful Katie today

I was born with Thalassemia, and when Sherif and I got married, he was tested because I had it. I knew that if we both had it, it would be guaranteed to be passed on. Since Sherif didn't have it, there was a chance both my kids could be free of it, but Jordan is carrying on the genes. Thalassemia is a blood disorder that is inherited, that causes the body to produce an abnormal form of hemoglobin, the protein in red blood cells that carries oxygen. The disorder can destroy red blood cells and cause anemia along with other complications.

One of the medical guidelines, if you have the disorder, is not to consume large quantities of iron. Regrettably, I was given liver as a kid and pumped with foods like this that are laden with iron that actually made me sicker. Clearly, my parents didn't have a firm grasp on how important following medical guidelines were. Since I did, however, I took great care in making sure to follow them with Jordan.

Unfortunately, more than just this blood disorder plagued Jordan as he was growing up. He was just three when the accident occurred. At that age, we never thought about the fact that he had suffered a massive head trauma, and to this day he has struggles because of it. Maybe we should have put Jordan in therapy, but this didn't occur to me at the time. I guess I thought at three there is no way he will remember it, but looking back now I realize that it could explain Jordan's behavior struggles and the mental anguish he often deals with. He was a happy kid until the accident, but afterward he was always throwing tantrums. No one ever said, "take him to therapy."

Jordan

While I was touring with Katie for her music, Jordan began to sew his wild oats. I left him in the care of my mom, but he was still acting out pretty regularly. Even at the age of 9, he started experimenting with marijuana. He was a brilliant kid that even started day trading at 8 years old. I started home schooling him too like I had done with Katie, because he just didn't fit in with school. Because he was being home schooled, it allowed him the opportunity to come with Katie and me while we were traveling for her music career.

Like Katie he was a great student getting straight A's, he was sharp as a tack! While other kids were playing video games, Jordan would be reading Barron's and giving me tips on what stocks to buy, but he was also smoking weed, struggling to manage his anger, and hanging out with the wrong crowd at school. Still, the born leader that he is, he was probably the leader of his bad crowd.

He was a talented child, always putting on skits for us around the house. He was helpful and full of energy. I focused this energy into soccer, football, basketball—whatever sports we could to keep him active. I put him in sports, hoping it would keep him out of trouble, but when there was too much down time there was time to get into trouble.

Jordan

Even now as an adult, there are times when he will say to me that he doesn't understand why he gets disoriented or why he starts doing certain things. Knowing what I know now, I believe that it could be because we didn't give him the mental assistance he needed back then. That is one thing I sincerely regret.

By the time Jordan got to high school, the drugs and acting out had gotten so out of control, I was lost for options. I had him Baker-acted and then managed to get Dr. Phil, yes Oprah's Dr. Phil, on the phone to ask his advice on what I should do. He recommended the Outback Treatment Center. This cost me another $60,000, but I did this to save his life. The initial things he said to me while at the center broke my heart. Saying things like "who does this?," "I'm not learning anything," and, "How could you do this to me?" But at the end of the treatment, and throughout this time of being alone in the wilderness, made Jordan independent. I strongly believe that he is so much like me: independent, strong willed, and dedicated to what he believes in. Nothing can change his mind, which is a tool of a great negotiator.

Then, when Jordan turned 16, it was a mutual decision that he move out on his own. First, living with his father, and then later on with friends. After living on his own for a while, the things he would say to me began to slowly change. Now, he said things like "You helped me grow" and "I learned a lot." It's funny when you think about it—both Jordan and I ended up living on our own at 16, albeit under very different circumstances. Jordan certainly got my rebellious nature.

Jordan

I will say this, Jordan has grown from a brilliant kid into a brilliant man.
Today, he is working for one of the top solar roofing companies in the
world, training his fellow employees, and people absolutely adore him.
Everyone who meets him just loves him, and he can do any job and
anything he sets his mind to. I can definitely see him as CEO of a multi-
million dollar company someday. Sometimes I regret that I left him with

my mother too often and did not have the opportunity to raise my child full time.

Despite everything, he has been through he has become one hell of a business man, and I'm so proud of him. I'm proud of both of my children. We have had our ups and downs, our arguments and makeups, but through it all we are family and are always there for each other. I have been blessed to travel quite a bit with both Katie and Jordan. My parents even took the kids to Greece one summer, what a great memory for them. I love my kids so much it hurts sometimes, and I would do anything for them. I know the parents reading this will understand—we just want our kids to be safe and grow up happy and be taken care of.

My handsome Jordan today

It may seem odd that I wanted to take a section and share about my children and their childhoods in a story about me. But to me, it's important to show that as we're trying to build our businesses that we all often still have things going on in the background. Everyone who hopes to start a business will likely have personal matters (raising children, losing friends, beginning and ending relationships, etc.) that they have to face or deal with. No matter what is going on in your personal life, though, if you want it bad enough you will make your business dreams come true. If not, you'll make an excuse. With that said, let's get back to my tale of reinvention of myself, as a sole business owner, without a travel agency partnering with me...

PART 5: MY NEW BEGINNING AS A STAND ALONE TRAVEL AGENCY

On September 1, 2001, I opened my new Elite Travel office after striking out on my own. I rented the top floor of a building, had 20 employees, and the phones were ringing off the hook until Tampa Bay got hit by a terrible storm. The worst of the storm hit on September 7, and I just had a bad feeling about my office, so I went to check on things in the middle of the night. It was still pouring rain, and when I walked into the office the ceiling tiles of the office were bowing under the weight of water.

The ceiling tiles came down, one by one, plop plop plop as we watched, soaked through with the weight of the water, destroying our computers and office equipment. If that wasn't bad enough, four days later our country and the entire travel industry would come to a standstill— September 11, 2001 happened.

I was in shock. I had just started my company, and everything froze. Every client called to cancel their trip. I called each one of my clients and asked them to wait 30 days. One woman's father worked in the world trade center, and she's the only one who, after I spoke with them, that canceled (her father was fine, she just couldn't bring herself to get on a plane for her destination wedding.)

I had 20 something employees and had to make sure they had enough money to live on. I wanted to make sure my best people stayed on, so I took an equity line on my house to float them through. Then, I just continued hustling. Many people would have closed up shop and given up at this point. Me? I'm a fighter and a survivor. I refused to lose any steam! Plus, I had the Elite Travel family to worry about.

Then, right after September 11th, sometime in October or November, the feds came into my office and asked me if I knew anything about the Bali Bombings. They told me that my company sold the guilty party their tickets and wanted to know why I sold them one way tickets. I also learned that the credit cards they paid with were stolen. The feds ended up catching some of them. We put a stop on the credit cards and canceled the tickets.

Sadly, when we canceled their tickets and gave the $21,000 back to the owners of the credit cards, the airlines wouldn't give us back our money. After that, no one was allowed to do international one-way tickets unless there's a visa or a return planned.

Luckily, better times prevailed and by the end of 2001, we were doing all the wedding shows we could. I met with Patrick McGroeder, the owner of *Perfect Wedding Guide*, the largest bridal show company at the time, and offered him two honeymoons for each magazine a year— 120 something trips, and I had just started doing honeymoons. Sandals said no, but Paul Pennicook, at Couples Resorts, agreed to take a chance on me. Even though at the time I had only booked nine trips with them. I learned that people win things for free and never claim or use their prizes, it's called "breakage." Paul believed in me, gave me 120 trips, and I became the #1 travel agent with Couples Resorts within a year. Couples Resorts was booming, and I had their name everywhere. Paul was amazing to give me that opportunity. I went everywhere and did shows, building our brand. Then, we started doing destination weddings more and everything was going great. This is back when no one was doing destination weddings, I was 14 years ahead of the trend!

- - -

Although things were going great in my business, as usual things at home weren't always wonderful. For example, one morning in 2002, I woke up to a crack from one side of the house to the other. The next day, it's even longer. I've separated from my husband at this point, and the next day the crack is even bigger. Inside the house, by the dining room, there was another crack that went down from the ceiling to floor in an upside down. I didn't know anything about sinkholes yet—I just knew that in my house the floor was slick and wet. I called an inspector, who sure enough, tells me there's a sinkhole under my house and there is a pipe broken and funneling water under my house, separating dirt under my dining room. It was empty under there, an underground cave caused by this broken city pipe.

This happened near Christmas, and my son was about 10 at the time, wondering where we could put a Christmas tree because of the large sinkhole taking up around 16 square feet. I did the best I could to get a tree, but the sinkhole pretty much *was* the focal point of the room for that particular holiday season.

Come 2003, my second divorce was finalized, and I was still pursuing my daughter's career. Around this time, I was working more and more with nonprofit charity events, garnering fabulous media attention and awards. I became one of the top agencies in the country.

Almost as soon as all of this success was bubbling up, the online agencies began making a splash in the industry. You know them as sites like Priceline, Expedia, and Orbitz. At first, it crippled our business and we weren't the only agency in trouble. Our corporate business slacked down and the recession was just beginning. So, we did the only thing we knew to do - we doubled down on our efforts to be the best agency we could be. We started price matching everything the public could find online, and continued to offer the best customer service of any high end travel agency out there. We also opened our phone line, so that we could run our business 24 hours a day, 7 days a week, 365 days a year to compete with the online angencies.

When we first began, we had three domains: EliteTravelGroup.net (because someone had the .com), HoneymoonGiveaway.com, and TripGiveaway.com. As the time went on, we continued to expand and evolve into the leisure and luxury business. This is when my strategic partnerships really blossomed and I began creating even more vendor relationships. The times were sink or swim after all, and I would stop at nothing to keep my business and my employees from sinking!

Then, we got a call from an attorney for NBC's Universal, and he said that we should do our own reality show called "Away We Wed". The first couple we had on the show was Marty and Amy Wolff from the show "The Biggest Loser". The idea of a reality show would fizzle out because the producers wanted more drama than I was prepared to display.

As I mentioned, my son Jordan was acting out a lot. He had a stint in juvenile detention, and during the show he got in trouble with the law again. As is common in reality television, the producers got really excited about this. They wanted the show to become a full display of the dysfunction of my family. I had no interest in this. A mother's job is to protect her children and I'll be damned if any reality show was going to exacerbate the situation by encouraging bad behavior!

Nonetheless, there was a lot of success coming my way. I was rolling in serious money, partying a lot and was very tied in with the Tampa Business Journal. Still, being by myself, running a multi-million dollar company absolutely on my own, all I think about to this day when I work is that I'm responsible for so many peoples livelihoods. I always make sure my employees get their pay. I'm acutely aware that I'm responsible for them, and that is what keeps me grounded and from going wild with spending money.

If you're keeping track up to this point, just since taking my business out on its own, we suffered a storm, 9/11, my own personal setbacks of a sinkhole and my divorce, but through it all I kept building my business. I was constantly doing bridal shows and doing as much as I could to help with charities.

One example of a charity I partnered with, was Ruth Eckerd Hall in Tampa Bay, to give back to the performing arts. During our partnership, they would give out my agency's information and a portion of the proceeds from trips booked from those referrals would go to them. Through my trip giveaways, and my charitable contributions, I learned the importance of strategic partnerships.

In fact, I've used strategic partnerships to grow every business I've ever owned. When done right, these partnerships cost you, the people you partner with virtually nothing out of pocket, and become the driving forces behind your continued growth for years to come. The first step to cultivating these relationships is knowing where to look. I talk extensively about strategic partnerships and how to make a million dollar business from nothing in my book _Starting a Business with No Money_. But the point is this—there are lots of ways to have a million dollar marketing plan on a shoestring budget. You simply have to think outside of the box, come up with new and innovative ways of getting your company name out to the masses.

One way I strategically partnered for brand awareness started in 2009. That was the first year I used my birthday as a way to not only promote a worthy charity, but also to keep building my name and my company's name so that people would know who Tammy Levent and Elite Travel are. For four years, I held an annual "Tammy Levent Birthday Bash" and raised money for The Friends of Joshua House here in Tampa Bay. These parties were very exciting and at one of them we even had celebrities like Sister Sledge, the Tampa Bay Buccaneers, and even the Prince of Austria in attendance.

A birthday celebration full of surprises and goodwill

The musical group Sister Sledge, with Tammy Levent.
BIRTHDAY, Page 4 center, performed at Levent's birthday party in 2010.

Tammy Levent's 3rd Annual Birthday Bash

Featured In: The Tampa Tribune

July 20, 2011

Speaking of the Bucs, when Tampa Bay hosted the Super Bowl, I got to do P Diddy's Super Bowl party at The Venue. Every way I could think of to help the community while getting my company's name known—I did it.

Jordan, myself, Mario-Max Schaumburg-Lippe the Prince of Austria, and Katie at the Tammy Levent Birthday Bash

Another reason I did these birthday parties is because in all my childhood years, my parents had never given me a birthday party. Talk about some serious emotional scarring. I always made sure while Katie and Jordan were growing up they got to have birthday parties, lots of friends, sleep overs, dance classes, singing classes, every sport imaginable for Jordan and Katie, and go to summer camps that were fun. I avoided camps that consisted of just baby sitting by another religious organization. This was crucial for my kids and my healing.

One of my birthday parties was the "Greek to Freak" birthday bash that raised more than $10,000 The Friends of Joshua House Foundation. I may start this up again someday, but time will tell. Basically during those four years, I got loads of media attention, gained massive amounts of recognition in my community, and helped a charity too. It was a win-win all the way around, and those are the best kinds of strategic partnerships!

I also expanded my company into corporate incentive travel, luxury travel and more. When trends were happening, I jumped on them, and when I wanted to get into other forms of travel, I created trends.

Birthday

From Page 3

ny grandmother always
jiving back," she said.
Levent chose Joshua
House because the children
have so many needs, she
said.
DeDe Grundel, executive
director of Joshua House,
said previous events, which
have netted about $10,000,
have resulted in school uniforms and shoes, new beds
and new bedding for the
residents.
This year the proceeds
will go for uniforms, shoes
and supplies.
"We consider ourselves
fortunate to be on Tammy
Levent's preferred charity
list, her support makes a
big impact on the quality of
services provided to the
Joshua House children,"
Grundel said.
For information about
the event, visit www
.tammylevent.com or call
(727) 726-9090.

2009, JOEL N. COCKER

Tammy Levent and Mario-Max Schaumburg-Lippe, the prince of Austria, take a moment to have their picture taken during Levent's 2009 birthday party.

Newspaper clipping from the Tammy Levent Birthday Bash

Nonetheless, destination weddings and honeymoons continued to be the bread and butter of my business.

In addition to working a lot more with charities, in 2008 I stepped up again—to get my name out there even more as a destination wedding and honeymoon guru by jumping on the Brides.com forum. I never pitched my company or tried to sell. Vendors were not allowed on the forums, so I didn't approach it as a vendor. I merely approached the forum as a way to communicate with people and answer questions. That is exactly what I did. I simply answered people's questions, built relationships and then if they reached out to me directly, I told them about my company. Some of my help went viral. Today, they call it content marketing, and it was this act of giving free advice that lead me to what I now lovingly call my half a million dollar bride.

Her name is Jackie Billy, and she has come to be not only one of my most profitable wedding clients, but also a good friend over the years. Jackie is from New Jersey, and at the time was studying to be a nurse. As a bride looking into wedding plans, she decided on a destination wedding because she and her husband were paying for it themselves. She started researching online and found a website that supposedly specialized in destination weddings. She signed up for $100, and regretted it instantly. She says, "it turned out to be a nightmare". She went on Brides.com to get ideas from other brides, and she had a lot of questions.

I came on the forum and started answering Jackie's questions right away. I never tried to get business from her, I just gave her my number and told her to call with any questions. I helped Jackie out of her nightmare situation, and because I wasn't pushy, but instead was helpful. She paid back the favor by signing with my company for her wedding.

I got her and her fiancé a great deal at Riu Ocho Rios, helped all of her guests in booking their rooms and travel, and as a result, booked two subsequent weddings from Jackie's guests—one in Mexico and one in the Dominican Republic. We've also gotten other clients from that one wedding that we might not have ever have met otherwise.

For a destination wedding, 120 guests is a lot of people, but by the time Jackie's 2009 wedding came to be, we made it as seamless as possible. Even when rain tried to ruin her day, we managed to get the hotel staff to dry off all the chairs, and the concrete walkway she would walk down when a dry moment came just long enough for the ceremony to happen.

What is the number one difference between me and the company that tried to scam Jackie? I genuinely care about the people I work with. I get to know my clients and learn about their lives. I stay in touch and form real relationships.

We also didn't charge for any of the wedding coordination, just the price of the travel and room to be there. All we asked is that her guests book through us—but they didn't have to. 99% did, but it wasn't a requirement.

The bottom line is that sales has changed so much since the early days where many people left the table feeling cheated. We're simply not in an environment where pitching works. It's important to become that trusted advisor and work from the heart, because those are the relationships that endure.

- - -

After nearly two years of giving away free advice on the Brides.com forum, I asked them if I could write a column for them. I have written for them, along with several other magazines, and although my topic is always about travel, the magazines aren't always centered on travel. Just a few of the publications I have written for include: *Destination Tampa Bay, Cannavoices, Regime Magazine, The Travel Institute,* and *Travel Market Report.* I've also been called on as an expert for *USA Today, ABC Action News, Bay News 9, Fox News, CBS,* and countless others.

I have learned that not only is it important to offer free advice, you have to tell the press you are ready, willing, and able to give that free advice to the masses. To further provide clients and potential clients with valuable information, I also started blogging on my domains. Not only does this bring in valuable traffic to my sites via search engines, it is teaching people things they may not have known about the travel industry, and allows them to share it with their friends and family. Whatever business you are in, you have to set yourself up as an expert in your field and then share your knowledge with the world.

With the success of all of my weddings and honeymoons, the writing, and my charity partnerships, I felt like I was in my prime in the travel business. Then, in 2009 a few days before my first Tammy Levent Birthday bash, another change came into in my personal life. I met a man that would become my husband, Robert, at a launch party for Ian Beckles' magazine *What's Hot Tampa Bay*. This was the first time I was dating someone significantly younger than me, but the excitement of this relationship was refreshing to say the least.

Although stunning to some, this relationship felt like I had finally found home. I had finally found my forever love. Our courtship was fun and just what I was looking for. He knew everything about me and my past and loved me anyway. To find someone who will be there for you no

Robert and Tammy, 2012

matter what is rare. On December 12, 2012, we married at what has become my favorite resort of the AM Resorts properties - Secrets Wild Orchid in Montego Bay, Jamaica – this would become my longest and most rewarding strategic partnership. As a matter of fact, because my dad Spiro was so ill towards the end of his life, Emilio Huhn the general manager of the resort walked me down the aisle. They have become my extended family.

Today, Robert is not only my partner in life, he is also my partner in business. He helps me in the day-to-day of running Elite Travel. The year 2012 would be the year that I would reinvent myself again, this time not just as an expert, but also as a speaker.

I began doing WhipShops™ to teach people in business how to market their own businesses with no money. I also started speaking at travel expos. You may be wondering what brought on this urge to teach. Well, to explain this I need to back up for a moment.

Remember in the beginning of this book I said I believe I am here for a reason? I have realized over the years that my mission is to teach people how to better their own lives. We must teach people what we have learned so that we can constantly boost each other up on the ladder of success.

By 2012, I was also starting to work with my daughter Katie, and frequently would bring up that I wanted her to eventually take over my business. That particular year, I brought her with me to an annual trade show for travel agents looking to build and/or grow their businesses. In one of the classes of 300 plus travel agents, the speaker asked everyone in the room to raise their hand if they were spending money to market their brand and their business. Out of all of those agents I was the only one who raised my hand. My daughter Katie looked at me and said, "And you want me to take over the business one day?" Another woman in the room said, "There is no money for marketing a travel business."

This wasn't the only instance of negativity I encountered either. Before this fateful event, I had been going to travel events for years and kept meeting so many people in the industry that were absolutely miserable.

Once the online agencies came around, so many agents were ready to throw away their businesses. Where most saw brick walls, I saw opportunities to re-invent. I knew that the online agencies would eventually screw enough people that it would come full circle. Whereas the travel agents like myself, that cared enough to stick around, would keep thriving. What people *really* want is top level customer service, and I knew deep down that everything would come full circle. Everything happens for a reason.

Realizing that I had built my business from minus to millions, I saw the opportunity to transition from student to teacher. I wanted more than anything to show agents that they could do what I did and be as successful as I have been. Agents had to quit thinking of themselves as just travel agents and realize that they are in fact travel entrepreneurs!

After the trade show, I approached another strategic partner I had worked with in the past, Kevin Harrington, an original shark from Shark Tank and the "Father of the Infomercial," with the idea of creating what would become my Travel Agent Success Kit.

His response was, "You don't see competitors reaching out to help each other every day. So when I saw Tammy's genuine desire to help struggling travel agents in her industry, I knew I wanted to work with her. I think her unconventional perspective on growing businesses is exactly what people need right now to succeed in this economy."

TRAVEL
AGENT
SUCCESS
KIT

So, in 2013, less than a year after that trade show experience, T.A.S.K. was up on my website for sale. Even though there were programs out there for thousands of dollars that don't teach nearly everything TASK does, I priced it low because I wanted agents to actually be able to afford the program to finally get their businesses off the ground.

Fast forward to today and T.A.S.K. is more than just a digital training program available online. Agents can still purchase the original kit online, but I have also expanded those teachings to include in person FAM trips with me at my T.A.S.K. Live events which are intensive trainings that break down the methods and ideas of the digital T.A.S.K. kit step by step.

Through my T.A.S.K. kit and trainings I also connect vendors and suppliers with the agents. I don't just make suggestions of the vendors to use, I actually introduce the agents directly to the vendors I trust and work with, so they can make strong partnerships quickly and easily. Unfortunately, 2013 was not without its own sadness. Spyridon "Spiros" Skordilis, master of the bouzouki, and the man I called my real father, even though he was in fact my stepfather, died on June 15, 2013. He was 83, and although his health had declined in the years leading to his passing. I mourned his loss greatly. He was a wonderful man, a fantastic musician and I miss him so much.

My mother and Spiros

Katie, Jordan, my mother, and Spiros

Interestingly enough, sitting at his funeral, I noticed something odd that struck me. I was looking over at my YiaYia's tombstone, and all these years later, it hit me that there was an error on it. I added up the years in my head and her tombstone said she had died at 78. Nope! She was 79. I told my mom and she looked me right in the face and said, "Only YOU would notice that Tammy!" Well, I had never had that much time to just sit there and look at the tombstone before.

With 2014, came a renewed desire to teach even more. I continued speaking at workshops and expos while selling my T.A.S.K. kit. This year brought about new and exciting business ventures as well.

My websites were producing more content than ever before, I released the book I mentioned earlier, *Starting a Business with No Money*, and I hosted my first T.A.S.K. Live event with Kevin Harrington by my side. I also started a consulting business on the side to work with travel agents, and some small business owners one-on-one, teaching them everything I know about how to run a successful company. I actually get into their businesses and tell them what they could improve upon and help them see the exact steps to taking their business to the next level.

The other big venture that came to be in 2014, was the launching of a charity movement known as *It's My Bag.* Earlier in the year, I was visiting The Friends of Joshua House and noticed that next to the kids' beds there were garbage bags. I inquired about the bags and was devastated to learn that those bags were holding the kids' belongings. The Friends of Joshua House is a foster home in Tampa Bay where kids wait in limbo until they find their forever homes, and it just broke my heart to learn that they had to hold their belongings in garbage bags because they didn't have their own bags.

As a member of the travel industry, I immediately thought of gathering donations of luggage, so that each child could have something to put their belongings in. I went to DeDe Grundel, Executive Director at Friends of Joshua House Foundation, and told her my plan and she and I discussed how to name this new charitable venture I had come up with. We took it to the kids to vote on and they chose the name *It's My Bag* as a testament to the fact that they would finally have something that belonged to them. I went to my creative team and asked them to donate their time to help me create a website, we officially launched the site http://itsmybag.cool/ in late 2014, and it quickly went viral.

Almost immediately, travel agents nationwide were jumping on the *It's My Bag* train and asking how they could help. As of the time of this writing, we have agents in eight states and in Canada collecting bags for foster homes in their areas. We are helping organizations worldwide including Eckerd, The Home For Little Wanderers, Silver Lining Mentoring (formerly Adoption & Foster Care Mentoring), and more. Amazingly, no money is changing hands, and yet we're helping so much. This movement is simply about having communities come together and give foster kids a bag. Some people even fill them with toiletries, new towels, and new sheets. I hope that this movement continues to spread and that every city and state starts collecting so that every child can have their own bag!

Finally, an interesting meeting happened in 2014 that brought a debt from my past to a conclusion. After the robbery in 1992, I didn't hear from the whole sale company, Continental Jewelers, that we owed thousands of dollars to for years. I eventually saw the new wholesale agent in 2002 and I said to him, "I still owe you money." The agent told me not to worry about it and that it had been written off ages ago. More than a decade later on January 15th, 2014, I was sitting at a *Perfect Wedding Guide* guild meeting and met the owner of the new Continental Wholesale Jewelers. His name is Andrew Meyer and once again, I mentioned the debt and he wouldn't take my money either. At that point I decided that if they wouldn't take the money I owed them, I would make it right another way. Elite Travel partnered with Continental Wholesale Jewelers to do a national Elite Destination Wedding campaign that launched on Valentine's Day. As I said, everything comes full circle and even though 22 years had gone by, I still found a way to give back to the company that I owed all that money to.

- - -

That brings us to today. Although not my most difficult year, 2015 has definitely been a year that I'll never forget. In early 2015, I was diagnosed with breast cancer. For someone who has been through as much as I have in my life, I was honestly taken aback by the diagnosis in part because no one in my family carries the breast cancer gene.

In the months leading up to my diagnosis, I hadn't felt well. I had been misdiagnosed for some pain in my back that turned out to be kidney stones. Even after those went away, I still just didn't feel good. One doctor appointment led to another and one test after another revealed what I already knew—I had breast cancer.

I'm very fortunate that the doctors caught my breast cancer early. I'm also fortunate that I was able to schedule a surgery to have it removed quickly. After the surgery, I opted for an alternative treatment that is not yet FDA approved. The alternative treatment I did is why I'm so much of an advocate for the legalization of marijuana. I wasn't smoking weed, but I was taking Cannabidiol capsules. The body has natural cannabinoids, and by giving my body additional CBD oil, I healed it naturally. The oil forced me to sleep 10-12 hours a night, which I *never* did before. Although, I do confess, one night I took too much CBD oil and slept 27 hours straight. That minor glitch aside, all that extra sleep did wonders for me.

Some would call me crazy for choosing this alternative method, but the proof that it works is in the results, I and people I know have experienced. As of July 2015, I don't need radiation or chemo. I will obviously have to keep being tested, and I am now telling everyone and their mother to get a mammogram, but I am in remission nonetheless in under 90 days!

My surgery to remove the breast cancer had its own complications, however. During the surgery, I began violently vomiting and had to be intubated. Alas, when the idiot doctors pulled out the tube they broke several of my teeth, cracking them down to the root. Why would you continue a surgery when a patient is violently ill I'll never know, but the surgery, the teeth and the recovery from all of it made for a most difficult summer.

Trying to run a business while dealing with struggles such as this, it's hard. I get it. What is sad to me though, is how many people I know quit when something bad comes into their lives. Running from your problems is a race you will lose my friends. That is why I am sharing my story. I have been through more struggles and tragedies in my lifetime than most will ever see, and yet I still have a great attitude and continue to look for the silver lining. When I can't find a silver lining I create one. Life is what you make it, and I choose to make mine great regardless of the odds against me.

You may have read this story and thought, "Wow, I can't believe she is still going," and trust me there are times I wondered how I am still alive.

But it just further fuels my belief that I am here to serve a purpose. I have news for you friends, you are here to serve a purpose too. It is your job to figure out what that purpose is, and then fulfill it.

After my first few encounters with tragedy, I realized that I have no control over anything that happens. I also realized that things can only get better, and that there is a reason for everything. Whether the things that happen to you are good or bad, you must embrace it either way and work through it. It will always make you stronger. No matter what, never look at any situation as a failure. In fact, I don't ever believe in failures, I believe in life's journey.

My plan for the future? My story is far from over and I have so much work left to do. I will spend the rest of my life teaching others worldwide how to build better lives for themselves. I will continue to train travel agents to be the best travel entrepreneurs they can possible be. I want to keep giving back to the community that has given so much to me, and I will be speaking globally to share my story of inspiration. I will keep growing my business until it is time for my daughter Katie to take it over, and even then I'll probably still be working up to the moment I take my last breath.

I also plan to take more time to travel for pleasure with my family. In the last few months, I've even been tracking down long lost family members. As I mentioned in the beginning of the book, my biological father left behind his 3 small children and his wife in Greece to create a new family with my mom and me. I could never understand how someone could just abandon their family, but he did it not just with them, but also with me and my mom without a second thought it seemed. Because he had another family, there are several people related to me I've never met, and I'm anxious to track them all down to connect and learn about who they are.

Believe it or not, as I was making the final edits to hand over this book to my publisher for the first round of printing, I received a phone call that my biological father had just passed away. It may sound cold to you, but I honestly felt nothing in learning he had left this planet. To me he was an abuser, filled with such evil. and I genuinely felt like writing some of the stuff that has happened in this book has been my therapy to get over my detrimental upbringing with him, and the tragedies that occurred thereafter. While growing up, we were taught to forgive and forget, and though writing everything here, and going through all I've been through has indeed helped me to forgive. Although I'll never truly forget how mean and heartless this man was to me and my mother.

The experiences I've been through have molded me into who I am today. I'm thankful to be strong and resilient, but mostly I'm thankful that I learned early on not to be an unkind, and selfish person that treats people badly due to my own personal demons. It is better to treat people with kindness and be a light of positivity in the world. This book was my closure. I'm also glad my biological father never met my children, because I didn't ever want them to feel the way I did until he left us. I can't remember the last time I spoke to him and that's just fine by me. May he rest in peace.

Interestingly enough, one family member I found is my great niece, Victoria Dennis, and she is a 13 year-old singer. Thanks to the connections from my days in music with Katie, Victoria is on the verge of a record deal. We're all rooting for her!

Now, it's your turn to answer the question that changed my life and lead me to my purpose! What would you do if money wasn't an issue? Once you have your answer, go do that. Are you ready? It's time to sink or swim and I hope you always bob to the surface smiling!

TAMMY LEVENT ACHIEVMENTS

- [ ] 2015 Gold Magellan Award for Travel Agent Innovation
- [ ] 2015 Silver Magellan Award for Travel Agent Training Program for the Travel Agent Success Kit (TASK)
- [ ] 2015 Travvy Award for the Most Innovative Travel Agent
- [ ] 2014 Saint Lucia's Top Producing Travel Agents for the 2014 Piton Awards Program
- [ ] 2014 Winner Travel Weekly Magellan Awards Honoring the Best in Travel
- [ ] 2014 Mentor BizWomen Mentoring Monday
- [ ] 2013 to Present Member of The Travel Institute's Professional Educators Program
- [ ] 2013 Debuting *The Travel Agent's Survival Kit™,* partnering with Kevin Harrington and GoGo
- [ ] 2013 Featured in the ebook *The Little Giant: Small Business is the New Big*
- [ ] 2012 Author of the #1 National Best Selling book *Women Who Mean Business*
- [ ] 2012 Named Ambassador/Strategic Partner for Business Women Connect
- [ ] 2012 Winner of the Editors choice awards for *Women Who Mean Business*
- [ ] 2011 Launch of the *WHIP It Out Show* (Women Have Infinite Power In Themselves) including WHIPshops™ and Seminars
- [ ] 2011 Featured in *The Crave* Book

- Advisory board for the Sustainable Entrepreneurship & Innovation Alliance at the University of South Florida
- 2011 Inducted and honoree in the World's Who's Who
- 2010 Made it to a Million Award – National E Women Network
- 2011 Speaker & Sponsor, 1st Tampa Bay's Women's Conference
- 2011 Women Extraordinaire Award
- NSA – National Speakers Association member
- Member: CLIA, IATAN, Tahiti Tiare Certified agency, Certified Destination Wedding Specialists
- Gourmet Inclusive Vacation Consultant for El Dorado Spa Resorts & Hotels as well as Azul Hotels by Karisma Elite Award Winner "Top 10 Selling Agency for El Dorado Royal"
- Official Travel Sponsor, Tampa PWG show sponsors, Elite Events in Atlanta
- Contributing Writer & Guest Expert: *The Perfect Wedding Guide, Bride's Magazine, Modern Bride, Florida Bride, For the Bride, The Robb Report, Conde Nast Traveler, Weddzilla.com, Tampa Style, Panache Vue, Pulse, Lady Angler, Travel Agent, PeterGreenberg.com, Orlando Style, Travel Weekly Spotlights, Tampa Bay Parenting, Applause, Choice Lifestyle*
- Platinum Preferred Agency Couples Resorts 14 years in a row
- Master Agent with AM Resorts
- Travel Impressions/American Express Vacations Global Award worldwide Best of the Best Agency 16 years straight
- Best of the Best Sandals Agency

- 2005, 2006, 2007 Fast 50 top growing companies in Tampa Bay (Only business to win 3 years in a row)
- 2011 National Diversity Council -Finalist Glass Ceiling Award
- 2002, 2008 & 2012 Business Woman of the Year awards
- 2008 Finalist TBBJ Ultimate CEO of the Year
- NBC Travel Show -Destination Wedding & Honeymoon Seminar presented by Tammy Levent
- Featured on NBC's Hollywood's *Extra!*
- 2001 to present Top 25 Women Owned Business, in the *Tampa Bay Business Journal Book of Lists*

The Entrepreneur's Publisher

75602727R00073

Made in the USA
Columbia, SC
20 August 2017